Dirty Motel Shenanigans.

King Chain Productions – Omaha

The following is a true account of events as they happened from 1997 until 1999. Names and business entities have been slightly changed and thinly veiled for legal purposes.

A note on the cover; the graffiti done by black marker is the authentic graffiti done by a customer tripping on LSD as described later in the book. I had the foresight two decades ago to take pictures with a disposable camera to document the art this customer did. I also need to thank Aaron Gum for his work on the cover, both front and back.

Other Works by Joseph William Simmons;
The Asia Diaries
Memories of Turtle

1st Edition © (Electronic and Paperback) April of 2023. All copyrights owned by Joseph William Simmons and King Chain Productions.

For Connie and Sam

Two souls woven into the tapestry of Life

Dirty Motel Shenanigans

Bonnie sat at her kitchen table smoking a cigarette. She smoked Dorals.

"Joe, you want a job?" Bonnie asked me.

"Yeah. Of course I do."

"Fill out this application," she gestured with a nod of her head.

I sat down with her son Allan next to her. Bonnie was a fan of potted plants; two or three of them adorned the table, next to her cigarette packs. Her motel apron was draped over the back of the chair I was sitting in. I filled out the application.

When I was done I handed it to her. She sometimes wore reading glasses that had a small dangling chain on each side, connected to a neckband so that they wouldn't fall off of her head. She hated wearing them – she almost never did – but she wore them now.

"Tomorrow you're coming with us for your first day of work. Be ready by 8:30."

Allan and I retreated to his room. I had just met him in the beginning of that summer of 1997. He was a tall, tanned, strong

young boy of mixed Swedish and Native Sioux blood that nobody
fucked with. We were always outside in the street playing basketball
and listening to tapes, blaring rappers like Ice Cube, Snoop Dogg, or
Westside Connection. Allan's mother Bonnie had been out of a job
for six months since the death of her own mother. She had gotten a
job at a local hotel at 108th and Q; her funds were depleted so she
applied for the Motel Shenanigans. She was the Head Housekeeper,
which meant that she was in charge of making sure the other
housekeepers had their rooms clean and ready for the next set of
customers.

"My crazy boss Arliss just got transferred to a Motel
Shenanigans in Texas," Allan told me in the comfortable seclusion
of his room. "On my third day on the job Arliss personally trained
me on how to clean rooms. We both walked into a room, and in the
middle of the room was a perfect pyramid made out of beer cans. It
was four feet wide by the base and almost touched the ceiling.

"Arliss was pissed because it was going to take numerous
trash bags to drag the cans out. We dismantled the beer can
pyramid; it took us about twenty minutes. There were a couple of
stray cans lingering about on the nightstand in between the two beds.

Well, Arliss picked up this can from the nightstand but it was still full. He thought it was empty, so he put more strength into picking it up than he meant to. When he lifted up the can, liquid sloshed out of the can all over his hand and that's when the smell hit me. It wasn't beer. It was piss!

"I smelled it first and when I did, I gagged. The stench permeated the room. 'Arliss, that can is full of piss!' I said. He took one big whiff from the can and gagged. It was so god damned funny.

"Another thing," Allan continued. "Sometimes…I listen to people fucking."

"What do you mean, 'I listen to people fucking?'" I whispered.

"You ever stay at a hotel, Joe?"

"Well, yeah. When I travel with my folks sometimes."

He got serious. "The walls are paper thin, Joe. Some rooms have a door that connects one to another. You can hear people talking, walking around, sometimes arguing…sometimes fucking."

I let it soak in. I couldn't wait to get paid and listen to people fuck.

Allan

I had met Allan through Tom Kasser, an acquaintance. Tom and I had walked over to Allan's house and knocked on his door; I didn't know that Tom didn't really know Al. He had an air about him when we were walking down the street that suggested he did.

Tom and Allan lived less than a block away from each other. Tom lived in a house on the corner, and Al lived just down the street. Tom and I were walking to the park when, right in front of Al's house, he stopped.

"Let's go say hi to Al."

"Okay."

Tom led the way up to Allan's door. I stood behind him. Al answered the door; he was tall, dirt blonde, and tan.

"Yeah?" He asked.

"Hey man, just seeing what you were up to. What are you doing?"

"Nothin."

I looked at Al's face and saw a subtle hint of confusion in his eyes. I could feel the tension.

"What is it?"

"This is Joe. You wanna hang out?"

"Sure. Come in."

I followed Tom into the house. Al's room was at the end of the hallway, to the right. The three of us went into his room. There was one window facing the street; light filtered in through the blinds. A CD stand full of CD's stood by the window, with tapes on the bottom. A large Entertainment Center took over the entire wall across from the door. A futon was across from that.

Allan had everything hooked up to the TV on his Entertainment Center. There was a Sega Genesis with its vast collection of games. A Nintendo Virtual Boy sat on a bookshelf. Under the Virtual Boy the shelf was loaded with VHS tapes. Tom and I sat on the futon. Al sat in a bean bag chair on the floor. It pillowed out from under him.

"What're you doing today?" Tom asked him.

"Nothin'," he answered promptly and abruptly.

We played Al's Virtual Boy for a short while before Tom and I left. Tom and I gave him our numbers so that he could call us later.

. . .

"What're you doing, Joe?" Al had called me a couple of days later.

"Nothin. What're you up to?"

"Nothin. Come on over."

"On the way."

I walked the twenty minute walk over to Al's, down Edgewood Boulevard. He answered the door.

"What's up, man. Where's Tom?" I asked.

"Whaddya mean?" He said.

"Tom isn't over here?" I said, confused.

"I don't really know Tom. Before you guys came over, I hadn't talked to him in a year or so."

"Really?"

"Yeah."

"I thought you guys were close."

"Not at all. Don't tell him I said this either, I mean I don't have anything against him, but I don't really like him. A couple of years ago he tried to steal some CD's from me. I caught him, forced him to give them back, and then I kicked him out. That was the last time he was over here."

I stared in disbelief.

"You seemed pretty cool though. If you want to come over at any time, feel free."

That cemented our friendship.

I began to see less of Allan six months later. Bonnie had gotten him a job at the Motel Shenanigans. He wanted money for a car. One quiet Saturday morning she took him to the motel; he filled out an app and got a job, starting out cleaning rooms. After two months Bonnie pulled Allan from cleaning rooms and threw him into a maintenance position. As a Maintenance Man he was responsible for collecting the Motel's trash from the public receptacles and making sure the walkways were clean. Sometimes he was given the additional responsibility of painting rooms. It was Al's idea to get me a job there with him. We were sitting on his futon in his room watching some old 1980's movie when he brought it up.

"You want a job, Joe?"

God. Those words. How wonderful they sounded. Job. Money. All I had ever wanted for the last year was to have a job. The only job I had had so far was being a paperboy.

"Are you serious?"

"Yeah."

I mulled it over. "Doing what?"

"Cleaning rooms, to start off with. After that, we'll train you in different areas."

"What'll you be doing? Cleaning rooms with me?"

"Most likely not. I'll either be in Maintenance, or in Laundry. You'll see me often, though. Plus I think I get to train you for the first couple of weeks so that you can learn how to clean right."

"How much will I make?"

"$7.00 an hour."

That was unheard of. Everyone at the age of sixteen started off at the bare minimum wage, roughly at $5.15. I was ecstatic.

"Count me in dude."

"We'll talk to my mom later tomorrow about it."

"Cool."

That night Al must have talked to Bonnie because the next day I filled out the app.

First Day

I was in my room anxiously waiting. Bonnie had given me a Motel Shenanigans shirt (complete with logo on the front pocket) and I was wearing it, looking out the window for her car. She drove a grey Honda Accord that didn't have power steering. That thing was a bitch to drive in the winter. I saw her pull around the corner and head up for my house; I ran out of the room and headed straight for the door. After she parked in the driveway I got into the back of her car. We pulled out and made small talk.

"You ready for your first day of work, Joe?" Bonnie asked.

"Yeah."

We drove down La Vista's familiar streets, 84th Street, Harrison, 108th. Bonnie smoked her Dorals and Allan sat in the passenger seat with his hair standing on end, a thin film of hair gel glistening on top. The window was down and the hot summer breeze blew in our faces. We went down 108th and took a right along the first exit you could reach before L Street. Winding our way through, we reached our destination.

The Motel Shenanigans was small and dilapidated. It sat between two large nice hotels that looked like hotels you wanted to stay in. As we pulled into the parking lot past the Shenanigans sign, we parked at the first available spot near the office. A swimming pool was by the entrance. We got out and I followed Bonnie and Al to a sickly grey-green door that was to the right of the lobby doors. The sickly grey-green door opened.

A man stood there. He had a gap in between his teeth with a goofy grin on his face. His face was misshapen; there was a weird dip in his skull near the top of his head, as if during birth he had slid out at a wrong angle, and the pressure from his mother's vaginal walls crushed one side of his face. He was balding, but his hair was slicked back Italian style. A lit cigarette was in his left hand. He looked like Peter Lorre on crack. He looked at me, not saying anything. Bonnie addressed him.

"Roy."

He let us in and we filed our way past him. In the middle of the room was a dirty wooden table. Sitting at it was a freckled tan woman with a protruding gut who smoked a cigarette. She saw me and immediately greeted me.

"Hey! Nice to meet you. I'm your new manager Barbie."

She had a deep, masculine voice that didn't match her face thanks to years of bronchial hairs growing on the insides of her throat and vocal cords because of smoking. She must have been a smoker for at least two decades. A child-bearing swollen stomach oozed out of her belt from her pants, contained by a floppy blouse. Al and I sat down at the table with her.

Bonnie went over to a desk against the far wall and took a seat. Roy walked into the Office; the Office was through a door to the back of the room. Through the Office door I could see a fax machine and a safe underneath a shelf. A minute later Roy returned. In his hands he had a large collection of papers. He handed me a small portion of the paperwork and gave me a pen.

"Fill this out."

The rest of the paperwork he handed over to Bonnie, who turned around and began organizing them. I scattered the different forms that I had received from Roy in front of me. Various legal forms were there, OSHA forms, tax forms, etc. Bonnie, sitting at her desk, took out a big yellow Word-sticker gun (the kind that you can type out sentences and it spits out the words on a sticker through its plastic mouth) and started making a sticker. I was working on the paperwork when she finished with her Word-gun task. She swiftly took her right index finger and thumb, grabbed the sticker, and deftly applied it to a nametag that had the "Motel Shenanigans" logo on the top left corner. She gave it to me. The name said "Joe." She turned back around to work with a collection of different worksheets that Roy had brought in from the Office. With her back to me, I lifted up a corner of the generic "Joe" sticker from the badge she had given me and read two letters engraved into the actual badge. I couldn't read the entire name of the person whose badge this used to belong to, but I could read the letters "AN." Most likely it belonged to someone who had found different employment opportunities in life, or who had gotten fired from the Motel I was about to be employed through. I finished the paperwork in 45 minutes.

"You know I have a fourteen year-old son that lives with me in the back," Barbie told me. "His name is Tommy. He goes to school in Council Bluffs but he is around your age. I've been doing this job now as a manager for around five years. I get transferred to different Motel Shenanigans as the real management sees fit but they've transferred me here after Arliss left around a couple of months ago."

When Roy handed me the paperwork to complete Allan had taken a set of keys from a cabinet in the Office across from the safe and walked out into the heat, leaving me alone with Bonnie and Barbie to complete my task. He reappeared in the doorway, keys jangling from his pocket.

"Is he ready?"

"Just about."

He sat down with me at the dirty table whose fake bronze legs had been eaten up with discolored rust and time. Bonnie had taken the paperwork that Roy gave to her earlier and separated them into different packets; each packet was attached to its own clipboard, with a set of keys. She gave me a clipboard with my own set of keys. "JOE" was written on the top of the packet. I looked at it. It was a list of different rooms.

"These are your rooms. Allan will go with you on your first three days to show you what to do, and what standards we have to meet to clean rooms."

"Let's go," Al said.

I handed over my finished paperwork to Barbie and followed him outside. "That's the Break Room," he said. "We'll eat lunch in there."

"Sweet."

I walked behind Allan past room 104. After room 104 there was a door with no numbers on it that was closed. Across from that by a large electric transformer was an open door. I looked inside and saw one huge washing machine, turning and spinning and spitting soap into a mass of water and clothes. It had a glass window on the front metallic door that you could see through. Across from that were two huge driers, commercial driers, with likewise giant metal doors on the front with glass windows that could see into the inside. To the right of the driers were the sheet and towel shelves; they were full of linens and towels. In between the driers and the linen shelves was a small space that contained two empty yellow carts. Above these carts was a laundry chute coming down from the second floor. The chute was nothing more than a hole cut into the floor on the second story, with a long rectangular metal box with open ends shoved through the hole. In front of the linen shelves was a curious looking device; it was a metal stand of some sort, with an inverted metal tip at the top turned downwards, and topped with a rubber piece. It stood five and a half feet high. It looked like a torture device, like a cross without arms.

Behind the washer was an open drain where the dirty water was released. PVC piping ran from the back of the washer to a metal trough covered with lime spots. The trough was slanted downwards on one end and emptied into another trough, running the opposite direction of the first trough. It was also slanted downward at one end, so that the flow of the water was controlled by gravity. The second trough opened up into an open drain that didn't have a covering of any sort. Next to the open drain was a table, a clean white table with a fake ceramic top. A sink and a bin with plastic legs and wheels were in between the door and the table. The bin was full of dirty wet rags.

"This is the Laundry Room," he said. "You'll come here to stock up on towels. Grab a fuckload before the Mexicans get here; they'll usually take all of the shit so you might not have anything for the rest of the day. First come first serve, dude."

I grabbed armloads of towels from the shelf and followed his lead. "Where are we going now?"

"The Cart Room. Follow me."

I went with him out of the Laundry Room. We walked back the way we came, past the transformer that stood outside of the Laundry Room, and went to the one door that didn't have numbers on it, the room right by room 104. He used his keys to open the door. There was no light bulb in this room; it was merely a dark, skinny, narrow closet that had built in wooden shelves that ran along the wall. We kept the door open to let the sunlight in. Metal carts with rusty shelves and big, black wheels stood across from the wooden shelves that ran along the other side of the "room." There was hardly any space to move in between the carts and the shelves. On the wooden shelves were Gideon bibles, ashtrays, soaps with the Motel Shenanigans logo on them, light bulbs, boxes of trash bags, and various other things that the Motel rooms needed but couldn't be found in the Laundry Room. Spray bottles with different colored labels lined the end of the shelves near the back wall. The color of the labels were Green, Blue, and Red.

"The most important thing to remember is these bottles back here. They'll be your disinfectants and chemicals that you'll use to clean rooms. The Blue Label you'll use the most; it's glass cleaner.

The Green Label is air freshener, and the Red Label you'll use once in a while to remove soap scum from the showers."

He grabbed and pushed the rusting metal hulk of a housekeeping cart out into the daylight. On the top of the cart was a carrying tray for chemicals, as well as a small compartment for the Motel Shenanigans soap. To the left of that was a pile of Bibles. Below this top shelf sat two inner shelves built into the cart. The top one was for towels, and the bottom one was for sheets. I was getting tired of my armful of towels that I had brought in with me so I sat them on the inner first shelf where the towels go.

"Yeah, it's pretty self-explanatory. Towels on top and sheets on the bottom."

"No shit."

He pulled the cart to the door of the Laundry Room, stocking sheets and towels onto it. He pointed out the differences between the different sheet sizes and assorted them into separate piles on the bottom shelf. After stocking the cart we rolled it to my first room. It was on the first floor in the Horseshoe area. The Motel Shenanigans was shaped like a "Horseshoe." More accurately, it was shaped like a square with only three sides. The open area faced L Street. Al

explained the terminologies and layout of the Motel to me.

"This area in here that faces L Street is called 'the

Horseshoe'. This motel is also known as an 'Outside Motel' because

the balconies and the doors to the rooms are on the outside, not on

the inside of a building or corridor, like most places."

"Gotcha."

We rolled to room 121, which was right by the Manager's

apartment. The manager had an apartment centered in the middle of

the Horseshoe. Room 121 was on the west side of the Manager's

apartment. Al opened it with his set of keys, and we went in. It had

two double beds with both beds' sheets tussled up. He led the way

and showed me around my first room.

"These of course, are the beds." He pointed to the two beds.

A fake wooden pressed headboard was glued to the wall above them.

He pulled out one of the beds; the headboard stayed on the wall.

Dust and lint laid underneath the area where he had pulled out the

bed. He didn't pull it out far, only around a foot. "You will need to

pull them out like this to make the beds. You'll get used to it." He pushed the bed back against the wall to make it look like a complete headboard and bed combination.

In between the two beds was a nightstand with an alarm clock and a Gideon's Bible on top. An ashtray was in between the Bible and the clock. Across from the beds on the opposite wall was an elongated bureau that had a desk on the end closest to the door. The bureau/desk had a drawer and under that, a dirty blue/green chair. The chair had multiple cigarette burns on the seat, revealing yellow padding underneath. The frame for the chair was made from the same fake pressed cardboard wood as the headboards to the beds; it was thick and sturdy. On the other end of the desk/bureau was a TV with wooden paneling. It was attached to a metal base, and locked to it with an internal locking mechanism on the bottom. A big ugly grey and black keyhole stuck out from the base.

I made my way to the back of the room. A door was in the left hand corner, jutting out from the wall past the beds. Allan followed me and instructed me over my shoulder, "This is the bathroom." A sink was against the wall to the right, and above that, a mirror. To the left of the sink was a shower with three Plexiglas walls, stained with soap scum. I could barely see through the

Plexiglas. Next to the shower was a toilet. It was unusually clean,

or at least it looked that way, right next to the scum-filled shower. I

panned my gaze back to Allan standing in the doorway, watching me

the way a proud father would watch his son ride his own bike for the

first time without training wheels, before he turned around and

reached up to the fan placed in the wall. The fan was in between the

door and the mirror, placed high and out of the reach of children.

The covering to the fan was yellow with nicotine. Al snapped out

the covering easily. It was connected to the metal frame of the fan

by two long double-sided metal hooks. The hooks were shaped like

hour glasses. He lightly felt the inner lip of the top of the wall that

was under the covering of the fan.

"Always check in here. Don't just start grabbing at thin air,

either. People sometimes hide needles in here. Be careful, and then

just take them out and throw them away."

He noticed that the fan wasn't plugged into the wall. Inside

of the metal frame to the fan, an outlet was reserved for the plug. Al

quickly resolved this by plugging it in. It whirred to life

immediately. He then took the fan cover and popped it back in.

"At the Motel Shenanigans in Brazil they have orangutan Helper Monkeys that do this," he said sarcastically.

He took me back out to the main room.

"There's a system that you have to follow to meet your time. They'll give you about a month to start meeting your average, but you're expected to do about 22 minutes a room."

"Wow."

"Yeah. You'll get used to it." He paraphrased to me the following System of Cleaning Rooms.

"1.) Take out the trash. The first thing that needs to happen is the excess garbage or any items in the room that doesn't belong needs to be taken out of the room, to leave you with bare-bones spraying and cleaning. This includes dumping ashtrays.

2.) Take out the dirty sheets and towels. This is a continuation of number one; anything that needs to exit the room needs to leave. There is a separate bag on the cart for dumping linens. The bag on the other side is for the trash.

3.) Spray down dirty surfaces. Mirrors, sink, desk, nightstand, anything that needs to be dusted or wiped should be done now as the particles can hit the floor for vacuuming later.

4.) Deep clean the toilet and shower, if needed. (Later on, all of us would always skip this step.)

5.) Make the beds. There are two sheets per bed, being followed by the unwashed blanket, and then the unwashed comforter. (The blankets and comforters around the whole Motel would be washed on average around once or twice a year. They needed it about once a month.)

6.) Stock the room with depleted items. This includes towels in the bathroom, the Motel Shenanigans soaps (two per bathroom,) light bulbs if needed, ashtrays if the ashtrays (two per room) are either broken or stolen, the Gideon Bible if missing or stolen, or any other items that the room should be stocked with.

7.) Check under the desk, under the nightstand, under the beds, and in between the mattress and the box spring for any hidden items, such as needles, knives, etc.

8.) Vacuum the room. After all is said and done, vacuuming the room is the last step, as dirt and soil that can be tracked in will go into the vacuum when you are leaving the room.

"Joe, I have to go for like fifteen minutes. Start cleaning the room and I'll be back. I have to do some rounds of laundry really quick."

Allan went off to gather laundry from some of the rooms and bring them back to the Laundry Room. I went back into 121 to clean it. I did everything that he asked of me; I took the trash out first. There was nothing in the trash except for an empty water bottle. I then stripped the sheets from the beds, and proceeded to carry the bottles with the Blue and Red Labels into the bathroom. The bathroom looked mostly clean as if no one had entered it. I didn't spray the sink down with the Blue chemical, thinking that it might not have needed it. Grabbing a clean rag I simply wiped it into the sink to gather possible water droplets. The moment I did, the clean abrasive fluffy side of the rag rubbed into something thick, wet, and stringy. Because I thought nothing was in the sink, I gave the rag swipe my full force behind it, but didn't count on the traction the mystery lipid would give me. My hand slid off of the rag and into the mystery lipid; I couldn't tell what it was but it was wet, gooey, and smelt like semen. I gagged slightly, turning on the faucet to wash my hands. I washed them with one of the unopened Motel

Shenanigans soaps that were left on the sink. After that I sprayed the sink down with the Blue Chemical. I wiped it out, sprayed the shower with the Red Chemical, wiped the shower down, and then went into the main room to wipe down the desk and night stand. I was done with most of the tasks related to cleaning the room (with the exception of making the beds) when Allan came back to check on me.

"What the fuck are you doing? Is this all you have done right now? What the fuck?"

"Dude...don't even say that shit to me right now. You'll never guess what just happened to me."

He looked puzzled. "What?"

"I swear to God dude, I just got my hand stuck in the sink in another dude's cum."

I explained in detail how I hadn't used chemicals on the sink when I used the dry rag, and wasn't sure if it was cum that I had touched. He laughed at me.

"Damn dude, that's fucked up. You're supposed to wear gloves when you do that shit. Make sure at least to spray the blue shit to clean it all off."

"Lesson learned dude, lesson learned."

He showed me how to make the beds for the room, pulling out the first bed and tossing a double-sized sheet to me. The first sheet to go down would be tucked in on all sides; the second sheet would go on top, covering the bottom and sides of the bed, but opened at the top. Then the unwashed blanket would go on the clean sheets, covered by the unclean comforter. The pillows with their clean pillowcases would go on last, but under the top of the comforter. The bottom corners of the comforter would be tucked into the bed with a stylistic fold.

After I vacuumed the room Allan followed me to the next room. He spent the majority of that day helping me complete my fourteen rooms (everyone else had more than twenty that day. They didn't want to overburden me.) It was the same thing for each room; take out trash, take out linens, wipe down surfaces, clean bathroom, stock the room, wipe down bathroom floor towards the main room carpet, make the beds, vacuum, move on, repeat. It went on that day for six and a half hours. At the end of the day Al and Bonnie drove me to their house for a chicken dinner.

The Third Day –The Anal Beads in Room 223

The next three days went by the same, more or less as on-the-job training routines. The rooms were either trashed or dirty, and Al was there to help and guide me. I used the basic system I had picked up on the first day. There was an art form in making a good bed. To have it done in four minutes was really a challenge. On the third day Allan spent more time away from me to do his maintenance duties so that I could build up more independence from him to meet the 22 minute quota. I was finding the quota impossible to meet. How did anyone do it?

I was placed on the second floor now. For the first two days Bonnie had placed me on the first floor as a courtesy, to get me used to the layout of the Motel and to the routine of the work. On the third day a Mexican woman who was seven months pregnant was given my former block of rooms. Bonnie was always trying to keep her on the first floor so she didn't have to climb steps. I pushed my cart over the dirty stained floor of the balcony to room 223. The balcony hadn't been painted in years. It was stained by the dirty water leaking from every other air conditioner that jutted out from the wall underneath the one large main window that every room had.

Roughly half of the units in the whole Motel worked correctly, but the other half were choking on the years of dust that had built up in their coils. Water mixed with rusty dust leaked from these air conditioners profusely. Permanent mineral stains streaked the balcony that wrapped around the entire upper floor of the Motel like Rorshach Blots dripped onto fine paper. The rickety wheels of my cart splashed through the tiny rivers of air conditioner water.

I made it to 223 and parked my cart. Opening the door, I smelled a peculiar smell permeating the room. I couldn't place it. I walked into the room looking for trash first, following the basic steps taught to me on my first day. Besides the beds being used, the room didn't look too much in disarray. The bathroom looked immaculate. The towels, soaps, and shower had not been used. I thanked whatever gods might exist in the ether for the unused bathroom. I walked back out to the trash can in the main room. In it I noticed an empty cardboard box; it was a box for anal beads. On the front was a naked man, well-built and oiled up, with his huge cock in between his legs. On closer inspection, the cock looked like an artificial computer simulation. It swung down below his knees and was too thick to be real.

I tossed it back into the trash, wandering around the room and gathering up all of the things that did not belong in the room itself. It was mostly a clean room; there was almost no trash besides the empty anal beads box in the trash can and some candy wrappers. Even the ashtrays were empty. I still was being bothered by the unusual smell. It didn't smell like cigarettes. The closest I could place the smell was that to a wet shit placed in the sun. I started to take the blanket off the bed. Roughly a foot and a half from where I had gripped the blanket I finally saw that the blanket was smeared with human shit. A thick line of feces trailed down the blanket neatly as if someone had wiped their ass with it on purpose. This was no accident. The source of the smell became clear to me in an instant. I analyzed the scene and realized that some human being must have had plastic beads shoved up their ass, and by pulling the beads out, the shit must have come out, too. I was still a virgin; I had never even slipped a single finger into a girl, let alone had experience with anal sex. However, I knew somehow that the empty box from the trash can and the shit-smear on the blanket must have been related. I just didn't know how.

I cleaned the rest of the room normally, putting on gloves and throwing the blanket into my linen bag on my cart. Then I phoned the Office to see if Bonnie was available. Roy told me she would be up to see me in fifteen minutes. In the interim I dusted, wiped, and made both of the beds (with the exception of the shit-blanket bed; I made that bed up to the point of needing a blanket.) Bonnie made her way into my room just as I was vacuuming.

"What is it?" She asked me.

I switched off the vacuum, walked past her and over to my cart, and reached deep down into the linen bag. I fished out the blanket, showing only a portion of the shit-smear to her.

"Where can I get fresh blankets?"

"God." Her face flooded with disgust. "Take it to the laundry chute and drop it in. Make sure it's wrapped tightly; we don't want people touching it. Then go downstairs to the Laundry Room. Past the driers in the corner there's a whole shelf of blankets and comforters. Only take from that shelf when you really have to. We don't have enough blankets or comforters to just replace every room with them."

I followed her instructions, simply dropping the shit-blanket into the linen bag and carrying the whole thing to the laundry chute. After I dropped the laundry, I walked downstairs to the Laundry Room. Past the driers in a small corner of the room I found the surplus blankets and comforters. There were no more than maybe ten comforters and eight blankets. If every single customer in the Motel decided to release their inner bowels onto our beds, we'd have a serious fucking problem. I grabbed a fresh blanket still wrapped in plastic and went back to 223.

The whole room was done except for the one incomplete bed. I threw the blanket on it and then the comforter, throwing on the pillows with fresh pillowcases. Even when I was done making the bed that damned smell remained. I thought I had taken care of it by dumping the shit-blanket. Getting down on my hands and knees following the source of the smell, I looked under the bed – and found it.

The anal beads were there. They were caked with shit. I ran back to the cart, put on fresh gloves, and ran back to the bed, reaching under the bed to pull out the beads. The shit rubbed off onto my glove-lined fingers. I fingered them bead by bead like a nun saying penance with a rosary for unholy thoughts. This was my first indirect contact with anal sex. "How did it make you shit?" I wondered. I had never even fathomed it before.

I walked out and put the beads in the trash but on the top so that Allan could see them. Coincidentally at that moment Barbie was walking my way. She smoked a cigarette.

"How's it going, Joe?"

"I found these in the room under the bed," I said. She looked into my trash bag and saw the beads, laying on top of the empty beads-box, complete with cock.

"Oh my God, I'm glad you found that in there," she said. "If one of our customers would have found that, they would have died!"

"Barbie?" I asked.

"Yeah? What's wrong?" She replied.

"I found a blanket in the room covered in shit too. I had to take it down to laundry. Why did these people poop everywhere?"

"One of the effects of using anal beads is that it relaxes your muscles. Fluids come out where the beads are placed in. I doubt these guys purposefully wanted to shit everywhere. They probably just accidentally did it when they were using the beads."

"Oh. Weird." You learn something new every day.

She brushed it off and walked back towards the stairs by the pool, leading to the Office.

The Towel Thieves

Within the first couple of weeks at the Motel my social

contact was primarily limited to Allan and Bonnie. During lunch or

in the brief moments in the morning when I had to stock my cart by

the Laundry Room, I was surrounded by the other housekeepers.

They were mostly Mexican women, but a handful of Mexican men

also worked with us. Two in particular, Jose and Aguilar, were

cousins. They had worked there at the Motel for about a year. Allan

got along with them the most. He introduced me to Jose right away.

Jose was a big six-foot tan Mexican. He wasn't fat but

stocky, brought on by good meals and a lifetime of work, and wore

his long hair in a braid that hung between his shoulder blades. He

was pleasant and cheerful. Al and I had lugged my cart over to the

Laundry Room to stock it up for my rooms. Jose and Aguilar were

both there as well stocking their own carts.

"Hey Jose," Al greeted them.

"Well hey there," Jose said back. He nodded his head in my

direction. "Who is this?"

"This is Joe. We go to school together."

"School, huh?" Jose chuckled. "I remember when I was in high school. That must have been more than ten years ago."

We all kept up the conversation as we walked into the Laundry Room. The Mexicans cleared out most of the towels. I was left with a handful of washcloths. I took them all.

"If you need anything, let me know," Jose said to me.

"Thanks man."

"Anytime, anytime."

He started singing a song in Spanish and then grabbed his cart, rolling it to the first set of rooms. Aguilar didn't say a word to me. He followed Jose the entire time until Jose left, and then grabbed his own cart. They went off in separate directions towards their rooms.

"Jose is cool as fuck," Al told me. "Aguilar though, I've got nothing against him but he doesn't say jack shit."

My acquaintanceship with Jose and Aguilar was short lived. It wasn't even two weeks after I had met Jose and Aguilar when I was in room 227 in the upper Horseshoe that Al ran in, out of breath. Sweat dripped from his face and soaked through patches in his clothes. He collapsed on the bed closest to the door.

"You alright dude?" I had just finished making the bed that he was lying on. The sheets of the second bed were in my hands. I was almost done with making the second bed before I had to move on to my next room.

"Jose and Aguilar just got fired."

I shrugged.

"Damn, what did they do?"

"They're Illegals dude. They used phony Social Security numbers to get the job here. I was down in the Office when my mom pulled me aside and told me that they were going to possibly be detained, and even deported. Barbie just got some kind of a call from an immigrations officer that discussed it with her. My mom was like 'Allan, watch out for those two in the next hour or so. The police are on their way.' I walked back over to the Laundry Room when I saw my mom walk out of the Office and go upstairs. She went straight for the block of rooms that Jose had. I saw Jose going back and forth in between this room he was cleaning, and his cart. My mom walked into his room with him and shut the door. She walked out five minutes after that.

"I then went upstairs to collect laundry. As I was pushing the laundry cart on the upper balcony I saw Jose and Aguilar running as fast as they could down through the parking lot. When they reached the wooden fence that faces L Street I saw them scramble over it and run down L Street in broad daylight, towards 96th Street.

"I went back to gathering laundry from the rooms. As I was pushing the cart from the inside of the Horseshoe and around the corner towards the entrance to the parking lot, I saw a police car drive up to the Office. I quickly finished gathering up the laundry and dumped it down the chute into the Laundry Room, then running as fast as I could into the Office. My mom was there with Barbie and a cop. Barbie and my mom were sitting around the table in the Break Room, and the cop was standing by the door, taking some kind of a statement from Barbie. When my mom saw me she stood up immediately. 'Allan, come out with me to the Laundry Room,' she said.

"The cop followed us as I walked out with her towards the Laundry Room. Parked near the Laundry Room was Jose's old beaten-up car. The cop took out his little notepad to take notes, and then he spoke to us. 'When I first got here twenty minutes ago I confirmed that the plates on this car are stolen. We'll most likely have to impound it.' He walked over to the driver side door and tested the handle slowly. It was unlocked. He opened up the door and did a general sweep of the inside. He didn't find anything.

"He then popped the trunk from the inside of the car. 'Step back,' he said. Me and my mom watched as the cop opened up the trunk and inside were hundreds of dollars' worth of our towels, dude. Jose had been stealing them for months."

"That motherfucker!" I said bitterly. I resented the fact that for the whole month I had worked here I had to continually run back to the Laundry Room to grab whatever meager towels were newly washed and dried to stock my rooms hours after the rooms were fully cleaned. Because we were so short on towels my average cleaning time had gone up because of the repeated treks I had to make to go to the Laundry Room. Even though a room was fully clean, we couldn't sell it unless the towels were stocked in the room too.

I imagined Jose and Aguilar running down the street at that moment. Who knew where they were? Did they run to the nearest payphone and call for a friend or family member to come pick them up? Or did they walk all the way home, plotting and planning their next move? Were they going to stay in the Omaha area knowing the cops might be after them, or were they going to flee back to Mexico? Their lives would continue elsewhere, somewhere on the North American continent. I was sure of that. My annoyed hatred over the stolen towels dissipated and turned into humor. Why the fuck would anyone want to steal so many towels in the first place? What was the point? Did they have some kind of forbidden underground black market audience that they catered to, hardworking middle-class people that needed stolen motel towels?

"I wonder where they're going now and what they're going to do," I said aloud.

"They'll probably go home and make plans for Mexico. I know I would," Al said in response.

I went back to making my final bed. At least this way I would have towels for my rooms now. For a little while, at least.

Ragnarok

Allan and I spent one of the last days of the dying summer in his bedroom trying to find a new way to pass the time with some form of entertainment. The movies, videogames, and TV shows that entertained us were wearing thin. We were playing the Sega Channel when he brought it up.

"Have you ever met Ragnarok?"

The name rang a bell. Ragnarok went to school with us. By the time he was thirteen he had a full grown beard. Everyone our age talked about his beard. He was partially Arabian with different European lineages mixed-in, but was mostly Middle-Eastern. He was a quiet, reserved, shy boy. It seemed like a deep contrast in between Allan and Ragnarok knowing each other.

"How do you know Ragnarok?" I asked him.

"Hell, I've known him since I was in first grade. He's a good guy. Do you want to walk up to his house to see him?"

"Sure."

We put on flannels and made our way through the heart of La Vista. It was a twenty minute walk up from his house past the conformed cornrow housing, all the same except for a slight color difference. The houses here first went up forty years ago in the 1960's as base housing for Offutt Air Force base. Middle class families now roosted within the homes, most of them never leaving the general area within the last two generations.

It was a somewhat chilly afternoon and the sky was grey as we went past the homes and a park, heading north towards 72nd street. After fifteen minutes we reached a complex of townhomes. I followed Al into a parking lot and up the steps of the last townhome tucked into the corner of the lot. He knocked on the door and I stood behind him; an older woman answered it. She had brown hair with wisps of grey intertwined. She looked tired.

"Oh. Hey." Familiarity was in her voice when she recognized Al.

"Is Ragnarok home?"

"Yeah. Come in."

She let us in and we headed up the stairs. The house was slightly disheveled and one could tell that a family of children lived here. Some must have been teenage boys. The floor was stained with dirt, mud, and pop. On the top floor, a narrow hallway led to a bedroom off to the end. Clothes were strewn all over the floor. We heard music and teenage voices coming from a door to our left. The door had a hole in it from where a fist had been shoved through, revealing the pressed insides of the inner door. Fake wood and cardboard was underneath. Whereas an adult could have punched his way totally through the door, it seemed as if a young teenage boy must have done it but lacked the full strength to complete the job. Al opened it.

A bunk-bed was placed against the wall. Facing one of the walls was Ragnarok, with a full beard, playing Crono Trigger on a Super Nintendo. Opposite the room on the other wall was a second television with a Nintendo 64 hooked up to it. Ragnarok's younger brother was playing some sort of racing game on the second TV. The room was full of half a dozen boys sitting on the bunk-beds, trying to look over the shoulders of either one brother or the other. None of them were playing the games with them.

"Ragnarok," Al greeted him.

"Oh hey, Al! Come on in man. We didn't know you were coming." He motioned for us to sit down on an empty space on the bunk-bed closest to where he sat. Al didn't budge. He just watched. I stood there with him.

"I'm so close to beating this part," he said to us. A little character (Crono) with red hair was on a bridge, surrounded by knights. He jumped up and brought the sword down on the bridge, destroying it. "This game is so fucking awesome."

He looked back up at Allan and saw me for the first time. "Who's this?"

"This is Joe."

"Hey," I greeted him.

"Nice to meet you, Joe." Ragnarok went back to slaughtering 16-bit demons with his party of adventurers. It was a brief introduction between Ragnarok and myself. After only twenty minutes Al and I turned back and headed out the door walking home in the oncoming dusk.

"That was so weird," I said to Al. I had never seen two boys playing two different game systems on two different TV's with a handful of others just watching and not talking.

"Yeah. Ragnarok's house is always like that," he said. "I'm going to ask him to work with us."

We kept walking down the street back to his house. Ragnarok seemed nice enough; a little strange, but those types of people were the most interesting. I couldn't wait to find out more about him.

The Vomit Caked Room – Room 124

Less than a week after meeting Ragnarok I walked through the front door of the Break Room. He was sitting at the table, filling out the same paperwork that I had filled out months before. Bonnie sat at her desk filling out her Housekeeper charts as Allan stood behind Ragnarok, looking over his shoulder to make sure he filled out the forms properly. Barbie also sat at the table with her small gut hanging out, smoking a cigarette. She was trying to get to know him by asking him questions about his life, his childhood, etc.

"So what do you want to do?" She asked him.

"I want to be an artist."

"Any plans after high school?"

"I spend hours drawing," he told everyone. "I'm going to school after I graduate high school, probably at an art institute. I'm saving up my money now though for a car."

I sat down at the table with them. Bonnie turned around and handed me a clipboard with a chart that listed my rooms on it. My keys dangled from the metal clip at the top. I unclipped them and attached them to my belt.

"It sounds like you have everything set out ahead of you," Barbie told Ragnarok.

"Ragnarok is going with you today," Bonnie said to me. "He's actually going to be training under you for around three days."

I stood up. "When is he ready?"

"Now."

Ragnarok stood up.

"Alright. We'll see you out on the floor," I said.

Ragnarok followed me out of the Break Room. Just like Allan had done for me, I showed Ragnarok around the Laundry Room. I showed him where to get towels and linens, where to dump old linens to be washed, and various other things he should be made aware of. I brought him to the downstairs Cart Room, followed by a quick tour of the entire motel. Eventually we made it upstairs to the Cart Rooms above the Laundry Room. Bonnie had given us rooms upstairs to complete.

"This is how we do it Rag," addressing him by his nickname and guiding him into a room. I detailed the System of cleaning the rooms; first the trash, then the linens, the wiping, cleaning, etc. He picked it up right away.

On the third (and last) day of training Ragnarok on how to clean rooms he received a crash course on how to be a lone housekeeper. We were both folding sheets and making a bed in one of my rooms when Bonnie came in to speak to me directly.

"How is he doing?" Bonnie referred to Ragnarok.

"He's doing well. He's got it all down."

"He's going to have to work by himself for a couple of hours. You need to come with me."

She was cryptic but not reprimanding. I didn't question her. With a wave of my hand, Ragnarok turned around and made the bed. I walked out with Bonnie as she explained the situation to me.

"I need you to clean one of Isabella's rooms for her downstairs. I won't let her do it because it might endanger her baby."

Isabella was seven months pregnant. She looked like she was going to pop. Already questions formed in my head.

"How can a single hotel room affect an unborn baby?"

"You'll see."

I followed her down a flight of stairs to the first floor, and then to room 124. Isabella was on the other side of the Horseshoe, cleaning a room. She waived to me. I waived back. Bonnie opened the door. We stepped in.

The room looked normal. The beds were already made, the trash taken out, the floor vacuumed. Although it looked fine, a smell wafted through the room. It smelt like bile.

"I made her clean this part of the room," she said to me. "Now let's go to the bathroom."

We went together to the bathroom. When I looked through the door, I saw vomit. Vomit everywhere; it covered every solid surface except for the ceiling and the upper walls. It looked like a dozen people intentionally and purposefully projectile vomited from the door, aiming at every indiscriminate object they could reach. The shower door had been closed; the only reason that the unused shower was clean on the inside was because no one from the night before had bothered to open the shower door before they had used the room as a human puke trough. Red and white puke covered the toilet and the toilet tank. It covered the whole floor by at least an inch and dripped from the sink, which was also thickly coated along with half of the mirror. Five inches of it had collected in the basin of the sink itself. Lumps of wet toilet paper clotted up into patches scattered throughout the bile, as if someone tried to clean it up but couldn't.

In my mind I imagined at least half a dozen people partying in the main room, with one of them being so incredibly sick off of too much alcohol (or whatever drugs they were getting themselves into,) that the rest of the group sequestered the one sick individual by himself so that he could detox. I imagined one person vomiting everywhere, unable to control himself. I saw this as a distinct possibility, but very unlikely. There was too much dried fluid here to only come from one person. I would never know the truth.

Bonnie snapped me back to reality. "Can you clean this? I can always get Allan to do it if you don't want to."

"No, no," I said defeated. The thought of anyone touching it because of my cowardice was unacceptable. I would be done with this in twenty minutes.

"I'll do it."

"Thanks Joe. You don't know what this means to me. You understand now why we couldn't let Isabella do it, don't you? I couldn't get her or her baby sick from being in here. Plus, she could have slipped at any time, possibly even killing her baby."

The overdramatic tone in Bonnie's argument was made real by the sight of the bathroom. I was going to have to find a way to keep from slipping in it myself. The idea of letting Isabella clean this bathroom just so that she could slip on some vomitus to murder her baby didn't fare with me either. If I had been in Bonnie's shoes I would have done the same thing.

Bonnie left. I went to the downstairs Cart Room and grabbed a carrying tray full of chemicals, a bag full of rags, and some rubber gloves for my hands. I returned to 124 to go to war with the Vomit Room.

Standing before the encrusted bathroom I dropped my supplies down onto the ground, and put on gloves. I was ready. Stepping into the puke and bile, I was being careful not to slip. I then made my way to the sink and scooped up the bodily fluids with my glove covered hands. I tossed it gingerly by the handful into the toilet. Five minutes into scooping, turning, and throwing the vomit into the toilet I realized the gloves were useless. The vomit on the counter seeped into the gloves from my open wrists with every throw, covering my fingers with a thin film. The gloves actually made it worse; the puke was unable to escape the confines of the latex around my fingers and pooled at my fingertips. It accumulated underneath my fingernails. I decided at that time to take off my gloves, wanting to just get this done as soon as possible even if it meant using my bare hands and then just washing them later with soap and water. Removing the gloves I threw them into the empty trashcan under the sink. By reflex I reached over to the handle of the faucet on the sink so that I could turn it on and wash my hands. I stopped myself before I could though. It made little sense to wash my hands now when I had an entire room full of vomit to lift and throw towards the toilet.

I cupped my hands together and dipped them into the sink, scooping the gelatinous fluid with my bare hands and throwing the scoops into the toilet. After I cleared out the sink of the majority of the mass, a small film remained. I checked the drain to the sink; it had been closed before the vomiting had begun. This further pointed to the maliciousness of the person or people that had done this. Someone had come into the room and closed the drain to the sink intentionally by pulling up on the drain stopper behind the faucet so that the puke wouldn't drain, which would let it sit there all night for someone to clean up. By doing this, it had actually made my job easier. If they would have puked into the sink without using the drain stopper, chances are it would have plugged the drain. I would have had to unplug the drain first, either with chemicals or a drain snake.

After I emptied the inside of the sink I turned on the faucet and wetted my hands. I took my wet hands and wiped down the sink in its entirety so that the puke-film washed away, down the insides of the unobstructed drain. I also did the same thing with the mirror. I repeatedly washed my hands in the sink to start off with fresh, wet hands, hands capable of attaching fresh red vomit to my skin.

The sink and mirror was done. I was going to spray them later with the Blue Chemical to disinfect them, but I still had to walk through an inch of stomach bile, food, and dried alcohol. I kicked my shoes against the wall to clean them. Puke dropped from my shoes with every kick. After doing this to both shoes I jumped out of the bathroom and onto the clean carpet. Small, oily trails of the aftermath in the bathroom wiped off of my shoes and dug itself into the carpet. 'I'll take care of that later with a vacuum,' I thought to myself.

I got down on my knees and placed the outside of my hands down to the ground. My thumbs pointed upwards towards the ceiling; I outstretched my fingers outwards on either side but kept my palms together, to act as a human shovel. Crawling forward slowly, I kept my hands on the ground, and literally pushed the pond of human waste towards the toilet. It rolled and swayed, but was thick enough not to roll back under my hands.

This took me an hour. By the time I was done with the bathroom, I had scooped, picked, and pushed a room full of liquid human enzymes towards and into the toilet. I washed my hands with soap. Streaks of bile were the only thing left behind on any of the surfaces. I walked back out to the carpet. I decided to bring back a mop bucket with a mop and bleach water to disinfect the room. The Blue Chemical wasn't going to cut it.

I left and returned with the mop and bleach water. By the time I was done with the bathroom, my knees and bottoms of my shoes were caked and wet, but the bathroom was bleached and clean. Not a single speck of vomit was seen anywhere. The bleach water was drying on the ground. I had won. I dumped the bleach water into the industrial sink in the Laundry Room. It was yellow and pink. After that I walked out into the cool air. My pants were wet but drying with the waste I had crawled through. Isabella saw me walking back upstairs to where Ragnarok was still cleaning my rooms. She waived at me.

"Gracias, amigo." The huge burden of her pregnant belly protruded out from her Motel Shenanigans smock.

"No problema, amiga," I quipped, and went up to Ragnarok.

When I walked through the door Ragnarok was getting done making the bed. He looked at me from head to toe, noticing my wet knee caps. He stopped what he was doing.

"What happened to you?"

"I cleaned a whole bathroom full of vomit."

I proceeded to tell him the entire story. To de-escalate from the whole thing I shut the curtain to the room and then advised Ragnarok to sit down with me. We didn't work for twenty minutes, as we watched TV and talked about ways to get some of the secret stars in Mario 64.

Hidden Caches – Room 215

The first time Allan and I started the idea of the hidden caches happened in 215. It had been my room. Sometimes, in the early morning, we would grab a laundry cart and push it room to room, stripping the sheets off of beds and grabbing linens. He had risen from mere Maintenance Man to running the Laundry. In the mornings (and throughout the day) he would make sporadic trips throughout the Motel, grabbing the laundry from the rooms so that we would have fresh sheets and linens.

As usual Al grabbed me aside on one of these mornings as we walked room to room, swiping the sheets and dirty wet towels. He liked to strip the rooms and get to them first before the other Housekeepers did; if there were tips or money left behind by the night's previous customers he wanted to get to it first. He never took my tips or Ragnarok's. Everyone else had cause for alarm.

We finished retrieving laundry from the first floor when we proceeded to the second floor. We grabbed a laundry cart and made our way to room 215. The cart was half full of wet towels from showered bodies and soiled sheets covered in skin cells and hairs. I used my keys to open the door. It wasn't an overtly dirty room. We stripped the sheets from the beds. After this I walked into the bathroom to retrieve the wet towels when I stopped in the middle of the bathroom doorway, dead in my tracks. The shower was full of ice and beer. The previous occupants to the room created a mini fucking igloo in the shower. It was piled knee-high, with portions spilling out of the door. Bottles of beer stuck in it like glass carrots in a farmer's field.

"Allan!" I yelled. "Get in here!"

He ran into the bathroom. "Eh ha ha ha," he chuckled. He ran out of the room and pushed the laundry cart into the room itself.

"Let's take 'em."

We reached down and plucked the bottles from the ice mound, stuffing the bottles into the cart underneath the soiled sheets. There was more than twenty bottles in the ice mound; there was no way we were going to be able to fit them all into the cart to transport them into Al's shitty hatchback without his mother seeing us do it. We would be ok doing that with maybe a few bottles only, but not with more than twenty. We needed a back-up plan. Al looked around the room, and then at me. He came up with an idea.

"Start pulling out the furniture. Look for places underneath that we can store this shit. We'll come back for it later."

I pulled out the nightstand between the beds. Behind the nightstand on the side that faced the wall, the fake pressed wooden lip connecting it to the floor was missing. There was a small space in between the bottom of the nightstand and the floor.

"Give me a beer," I said.

He tossed me a wet, cold bottle. I tried fitting it underneath the nightstand but the space wasn't big enough. The fat bulge of the body of the bottle clinked against the base.

"Shit. This isn't going to work."

Al looked around the room. The only other piece of furniture besides the chair and beds was the huge desk/bureau that the TV was fastened to.

"Hold on."

He went over to the side of the desk/bureau where the TV was and lifted it, pulling it out slightly. Like the nightstand, the back of the desk/bureau had a missing backside. The desk/bureau was bigger than the nightstand, however. I tossed him the same beer that he had tossed to me a moment ago, and he slid it into the empty

space. It fit.

"Get more," he said to me.

We both rushed into the bathroom and took as many beers as

we could carry, fitting them underneath the TV section of the

desk/bureau to full capacity, and then slid the TV back against the

wall. The bottles clanked restlessly for 3 seconds before coming to a

halt. They were hidden perfectly.

"We're going to have to remember to check behind the TV's

once in a while," he thought out loud to me. "What if other people

hid shit in other rooms like this, and we didn't bother to check?"

We sat down and cracked beers open, turning on the TV and

sitting on the unmade beds, drinking. Flipping through the channels,

we had a choice in between the Teletubbies or CNN. We chose the

Teletubbies. After finishing our beer Al left with the remnants of his

treasure trove of bottles hidden underneath dirty sheets in the

laundry cart. He went about completing the double task of collecting

more sheets, and to wait for Bonnie to be out of sight so that he

could hide the bottles in the trunk of his car. I went on about my

business, cleaning room 215 so that an unknowing customer could stay in what looked like a clean room, but was really a cache of

hidden beers for underage boys.

Connecting Rooms – Listening to the Sounds of Fucking in 224

Our motel had "Connecting Rooms." If two or more families wanted adjoining rooms, some of the rooms were connected on the wall across from the bathroom by a set of doors that had to be unlocked from the inside. By gaining access to both neighboring rooms from the inside, the related parties could gain access to each other's room by walking through the unlocked doors. The problem was these doors were not insulated in between each other (they couldn't be.) Unlike the insulated walls that at least muted sound because of their thickness, the rooms with the Connecting Doors were perfect purveyors of sound. Complete strangers could listen to each other shitting, eating, laughing, crying, watching TV, or fucking very clearly, especially if someone put their ear up to the door connecting the rooms.

I was downstairs with a block of first floor rooms by the pool doing the usual; making beds, dumping trash. After a steady summer of work, school was now in session and we were all forced to work on the weekends. Al and I wanted more hours so sometimes we worked the desk during the evenings after school. On this

Saturday two weeks after I had become a Junior in high school I was cleaning one of my rooms when he came running into my room.

"Joe. Come with me man. People are fucking."

I dropped my bottle of Blue Chemical on the desk and ran out after him. We bolted up the rusty, crumbling stairs by the pool to the second floor and ran down the balcony above the Manager's Apartment as fast as we could. We ran to room 224. He put his finger to his lips to signal for silence, deftly sliding the key into the key hole and turning the knob all the way to the right so that the door latch would be totally withdrawn into the door. This way it would not make a sound as it slid across the metal latch frame.

We opened the door. It was a clean room that smelled like the cheap Green Chemical. Allan tiptoed to the door connected to the wall and beckoned with his finger for me to follow. I did so. He put his ear to the door, and I did the same. Then we heard it.

"Ahhh...ugh...ah...ahhhh..."

A woman was moaning. We couldn't hear the man; we didn't want to. The woman was getting fucked and that's all we cared about. She was getting fucked next door on washed sheets under an unwashed blanket and bedspread. Al kept his voice down real low.

"They've been doing this for a while."

A light bulb went off in my head.

"We have to go get Ragnarok."

"You're right," he affirmed.

We slunk out of the room as quietly but as quickly as we could. We ran out, keeping the door cracked open slightly so that sound could be minimized upon return.

"Where the fuck is he?" I said.

"I don't know."

"What, aren't you in Laundry today? How come you don't know?"

"I've been in Maintenance. I haven't seen him all day."

"Fuck."

We ran around the balcony out of the Horseshoe and down the south side of the Motel. Ragnarok was downstairs at his cart, wiping out an ashtray. I pointed.

"THERE!"

We headed towards the stairs and ran down to Ragnarok. He stopped wiping out the ashtray.

"What's going on?" He said with concern.

Al cut right in. "People are having sex upstairs."

He tossed the ashtray and his rag on the top of his cart. All three of us sprinted back up the dirty stairs and ran back to 224. Just like before Al brought his finger to his lips as we trailed behind him, slowing our pace. He opened the door and all three of us went in. We walked over to the Connecting Door, making room for each other like hungry pigs diving for swill and put our ears to the door. Silence.

"Are they done?" Ragnarok said at room level. Immediately Al put his finger yet again up to his lips and "shhh'd!" him. Then a faint noise wafted through the door.

"Ugh…ahhh…"

I looked over at Al and Rag. Ragnarok's mouth was open. His tongue was hanging out, quivering in anticipation of hearing penetration. I wondered what I looked like. I must have looked as silly as they did. Slight moans were heard. They weren't as loud as before. They were less animated. The man on top must have slowed down from exasperation. For all we knew, the woman was in there by herself, banging herself with her fingers or dildo or cucumber. We might have been listening to a lone woman pleasuring herself. When all you hear is the alto or soprano squealing of a woman's pleasured voice, she already forms the image of being a supermodel. It could have been a number of scenarios. She could have been in there surrounded by six guys jerking off over her and dressed up like mimes while a dwarf had his way with her. All we heard was her.

We listened to her sex sounds like that for about ten minutes with our ears pressed up to the door. We were pretty sure she was done when we heard the patter of feet in the bathroom. Either the woman was using the bathroom to air out her snatch, or the man she was with was emptying his condom into the toilet. When we were sure the fucking had stopped the three of us sat down on the beds. Since we had gotten what we had come for we no longer worried about proceeding in hushed undertones, so we turned on the TV.

"I'm going to make a list of all the rooms that have Connecting Doors like this one," Al said before Rag and I left.

"That's a great idea," I said.

Ragnarok and I left Allan there to sit and watch TV while we walked back to our rooms.

Dickens

Dickens' mother was Filipina. His father was an American that met his mother in the Philippines when he was in the Air Force back in the early 70's. Dickens' father brought back his mother to the States and they had Dickens' older brother Thames a couple of years later. They moved into a quaint little house in La Vista with a huge pine tree in front.

In the early 80's they had Dickens. Now, seventeen years later, Dickens was a tall young man with a bowl cut. His black shiny hair was matted down on top and cut in at the middle of his skull. From the ears down he was shaved bald to the skin.

Allan had known Dickens since they were kids. They had met in first grade and had been friends ever since. They used to have slumber parties up until Al was nine years old. The last time he had slept over at Dickens', Dickens' parents got into a vicious fight, which included Dickens' mother breaking several dishes and bottles thrown at her husband. Bonnie had to go up to Dickens' house to get Al.

Dickens and Al were still close after that incident. When we were Juniors in high school, Dickens, Allan, and even Turtle had the same anthropology class. One day, after months of regaling both

Dickens and Turtle with tales from the Motel Shenanigans, Al

leaned over to Dickens and asked him,

"You want a job, Dick?"

"With you? Of course I do," he said.

That's how I met Dickens in a formal capacity. I went to

work as usual on a Saturday and Dickens was in the Break Room,

filling out new hire paperwork. I sat down by him. Through Allan I

had a mere acquaintance with Dickens but I still didn't know him

well.

"What's up, Dickens?"

"What's up Joe."

Bonnie was sitting at her desk making the Housekeeping

charts. She addressed me.

"He's training with you to start off with Joe. Your average

room time might go up but Allan will pop in from time to time to

help you."

"You're the boss."

I waited for Dick to get done with his papers. After that I led

him outside to the Laundry Room. After showing him around the

Laundry and Cart Rooms, we stocked our cart with the various things that we were going to need. We were working on our second room together when Al came into the room. He turned on the TV and sat down. Dickens sat down on the other bed. I sat in the chair.

"What do you think of your first day?" Al asked him.

"Fuckin' chill, man."

Al then proposed a bold idea to us. It had been gaining momentum before Dickens had been hired, when Ragnarok started after I did. The seeds of this idea were then planted, but not yet fully formed, until Dickens' employment.

"I'm going to get everyone to work here with us. Like ten of us from school," he said.

It was such a subtle idea. It was also very powerful. We had never before stopped to think that at this seedy commercial motel, where we had the power to influence management through Al's mother, that we could build a small army of friends to work and experience all kinds of shit. Dickens picked up on it first.

"Like who?"

"Turtle," Al suggested.

Turtle was known as a junkie throughout school. Mostly he was a pothead but he was known to have done almost every drug known to man by the time he was sixteen. He was also a huge acid freak. One could only guess what was going to happen if he started working here.

"Who else?" I asked this time.

"Hel. Hel Samwig," Al said.

The name was infamous at Papio. Hel was a tall, built, crazy motherfucker. He lived on a farm near Plattsmouth but commuted every day to go to school, and had a blue Ford F-150 that had a rusting truck bed. He chewed tobacco on a regular basis; his truck always had an empty plastic soda bottle filled with spat chew congealing on the bottom. One time Hel and a close friend of his were playing a videogame when his friend made the mistake of reaching over and grabbed Hel's chew bottle, mistaking it for his own soda. He drank deep and swallowed before he gagged and choked out Hel's spat chew in a dry heave. Hel went wild with laughter for twenty minutes when it happened. I had never met Hel before. Al and Hel had a Home Economics class together. They were assigned in the same group for a semester to bake pies.

"I'll talk to Turtle and Hel as soon as I see them in school," Al said.

An idea came to me.

"What about Mac Whiane?" I asked. Mac was another good friend of ours, one that dropped out of high school and sat around smoking weed all day.

"Good idea. You call him and I'll work on Turtle and Hel."

We sat and watched TV for fifteen minutes before Al stood up to leave. Dickens and I turned back to work. In our three heads we were preoccupied with getting our plan into action.

Turtle (And Long's Diatribe)

Turtle was adopted by his parents when he was young. They couldn't have children of their own, so they adopted Turtle and Turtle's older sister, Jane. Jane was an overachiever. She was in sports all throughout junior high and high school. In their basement, various awards depicting Jane's successes in school and in Girl Scouts dotted the wall by the family laundry room. In contrast, Turtle's two displayed awards dated back to elementary school when he was in Cub Scouts. Turtle and his dad entered into a Father/Son create-your-own wooden racing boxcar competition known to the Scouts as the Pinewood Derby. They did that for two years, and Turtle placed highly in some long-forgotten division. The awards were remnants of a dead past. They remain on the wall to this day.

Turtle stopped caring about Life when he was roughly fourteen years old. This is when I first met him; my neighbor was friends with Turtle. For my neighbor's fourteenth birthday we ended up playing baseball and camped out in my neighbor's backyard with him. Turtle was clean back then. When I first met him the most he had done was smoke a cigarette. It was only months after I had met him that he started experimenting with weed and LSD.

Turtle's mom found LSD in his room when he was fourteen years old, and committed him to a now defunct mental health hospital in downtown Omaha. He was there for one week. After his release, he still took weed and LSD regularly, and graduated to other chemicals like mushrooms and opium. He started smoking a pack a day when he was fifteen years old.

There was this old gas station that used to be on the southeast corner of 72nd and Harrison called Long's. When Turtle was fourteen he would walk down to Long's to buy his cigarettes. A local family ran the store; it was owned by a beard-sporting hippy named Ajax and his decrepit mother, who was in her early 80's. Ajax was a mechanic who was usually in the back working on cars while his mother ran the counter. The gas station was full of garbage; Ajax was a hoarder, and his mother was too old to do anything except count change. She looked like a wrinkled human lizard forever stuck in the decade of the 70's.

Phone books, invoices, tools; piles of garbage, some useful, most not, were stacked and heaped on the floor to the ceiling. Skinny narrow passageways were dug out and through the trash pile that was Long's to make trails for people to reach the counter.

Turtle would make his way to the counter and wait for any nearby adult customers to be out of earshot before he would ask in a low, hushed voice,

"Can I have some Marlboro Reds?"

And Ajax's mother would also keep her eyes open on any nearby adults. She would take Turtle's money and slide a pack of Red's to him as swiftly as if the transaction was a ghost.

I went there one time with him right before he started working at the Motel. We were sixteen years old, both of us, and I had just started driving. I took him there because I wanted a pack of Newports. Turtle promised me that someone of age would sell to us without any questions. I pulled up to the nasty rotten gas station with Turtle in my Eurosport. Three old fashioned gas pumps from the 50's stood in the middle of the small broken and cracked parking lot. They had the old fashioned glass bulb meter on the top of the pumps with a needle to show how much gas you were pumping. Turtle and I got out and went into Long's. I noticed parts of the wall outside of the door were missing, revealing studs underneath. It looked like rats had chewed their way through it. We walked in and the rank smell of decaying paper hit my nostrils. There was a man in a business suit going through some invoices at the far side of the station. I could barely see his upper half through the trash. We made our way up to the counter. I was nervous; I didn't know this lady at all.

"Can I have some Red's?" Turtle asked. Ajax's mother put her skeletal finger to her lips.

"Wait until he leaves, son." She gestured to the man in the suit by the window.

We stood back away from the counter for five minutes. Other adult customers came in and paid for their gas in cash (Long's hadn't entered the modern age of accepting credit cards.) Finally the loitering Business Man came to the counter, dropped some papers and a $20 bill, and walked out. Mrs. Long gestured with her old, quivering hand. 'Come here,' it beckoned. She accepted our cash and got our packs of smokes for us.

"Now you boys, if you come back in here, wait for the adults to leave. I don't want to get into any trouble."

"Sure thing, Mrs. Long," Turtle said apologetically.

Triumphant we left with our respective packs and lit up in my vehicle. Shortly after this, Long's would end up losing their tobacco license after Mrs. Long sold a pack to a kid, and that kid's parents turned her and the station into the police. After that happened though, Turtle and I would always go back to Long's for our cigarettes; Ajax and Mrs. Long stored cartons of cigarettes in the trunk of a broken-down car in the back of the shop. We were only permitted to go there after hours when everyone else was gone and buy packs from her then. We would stand near broken vehicles and mounds of tools covered in oil like choir boys receiving a dirty communion with the allure of cigarettes in the air.

Long's was finally closed because the building was condemned at the turn of the century. Ajax made the news on the final day of the Family Business; three cop cars pulled in one day to hand Ajax his eviction notice served to him by the City of La Vista. He went crazy and grabbed a gas can, doused all three cruisers with gas, and poised over one of them with his lighter, ready to strike. The three policemen tackled him and hauled him off to jail. Long's was torn down three years after his arrest, a vacant skulking mass that rotted there on the corner until the bulldozers came in.

Losing Long's was the end of an era.

...

I was in Allan's room at his house when he told me that

Turtle was going to start work with us.

"No shit?" I said, ecstatic.

"No shit."

"What'd your mom say about it?"

"She said it was cool."

"Cool."

"He starts this Saturday."

I walked into the Break Room on Saturday to begin work as a

housekeeper. Allan, Ragnarok, and Dickens sat around the table as

usual waiting for the instructions for our duties of the day, but Turtle

was also there, smoking a Marlboro Light, smoky curls lifting off of

the tip. Bonnie sat at her desk. I thought it was such a bold move

for Turtle to just light up in the Break Room on his first day of work,

being underage. I didn't know if he asked Bonnie if he could, and I

didn't ask. I squeezed myself into whatever meager space was left

around the tiny table.

"Allan and I will train him today," Bonnie said to me. "You

might have him later on in the week."

That was fine with me. Now I could keep my average room quota by not being slowed down. I was just glad he was here.

Mac Whiane

Winter approached yet the snows still had not come. Turtle's parents had let him borrow their wood-paneled station wagon that had been his grandfather's vehicle back in the 60's. I usually had either the option of riding with Bonnie and Al, or Turtle. It wasn't a problem for me to ride with Bonnie and Al of course, but if Turtle picked me up he always had cigarettes on him, and we would smoke three or four before making it to work. I preferred Turtle's company because I wanted to feed my nicotine monkey before I turned to cleaning rooms. Besides, the conversation was also more involved, usually involving the crazy drugs or the strange shit Turtle had gotten into the day or week before.

Turtle was slated to pick me up on this particular morning so I waited for him patiently. I was playing Final Fantasy 6 on my Super Nintendo (the wages from the Motel had let me afford an entertainment center, a Nintendo 64, and funds to afford the library of games I was building for the SNES.) I had just gotten to Kefka when I heard the low rumble of an old motor in my driveway. I looked out the window and saw Turtle behind the wheel. I shut off the SNES and ran out into Turtle's parents' station wagon.

"You got a smoke?" I said.

Turtle whipped out a pack of Newports. I took one and lit it up as soon as we were down the street out of view of my parent's house.

"What up, man?" I asked.

"Nothin'much." A cigarette dangled from Turtle's lips.

"Hey, earlier this month Al and I have been talkin'," referring to the small meeting in between Allan, Dickens, and I held earlier. "We're thinking of asking Mac Whiane and Hel Samwig to work with us at the Motel."

"No shit." Turtle's lips were drawn into a tightly clenched smile to hold the cigarette he was smoking in his mouth.

I was under the assumption that I would be responsible for asking Mac Whiane about the proposition to work with us. I had lost Mac's phone number, so my plans of calling him were delayed. My only chance of communicating our intentions to him was to stop by his house and discuss it with him. Mac had dropped out of school and smoked pot in his basement every day. It was going to be a bitch to get a hold of him now.

A week after Turtle and I discussed Mac Whiane getting a job with us, Bonnie and Al came to pick me up for work. I got into Bonnie's grey Honda and slid into the back. I was fiending for a smoke but I never dared to ask Bonnie for one. We pulled out and were on Park View when Al brought it up.

"Mac Whiane starts work at the Motel today."

"Really?"

"Yeah."

"How did he know?"

"I guess Turtle talked to him about it. Mac called me last night."

Bonnie jumped in. "I told him to be there this morning to start."

"Cool."

"You kids have school so it's difficult for us to staff the Motel during the week, but Mac's looking for work every day. We could use a kid like that." Bonnie had already known about Mac dropping out of school.

We pulled up to the Motel and parked. Walking in I saw Mac already at the table in the Break Room.

"Mac, you'll be training with Joe today." Bonnie made the announcement and sat at her desk to prepare the charts.

I couldn't wait to get Mac aside and talk to him. It had been months since I had seen him last. Bonnie worked on my chart first so that we could both get started. She made some adjustments to the piece of paper that was going to be my block of rooms, walked over to retrieve the keys, and then came back over to me handing me both.

"Get started."

Mac and I walked out of the Break Room. I went through the spiel of where to get supplies, how to stock a cart, etc. After we stocked up on towels and linens, I pushed the cart with Mac behind me to our first room, which was right next door to the Laundry Room. I opened it to begin the ritual of training on the first day. After I had walked in Mac walked in past me. I noticed the smell of weed on him. It was for the briefest of moments but I caught a glimpse of Mac's eyes; they were red and blood shot.

"Are you stoned, Mac?" I asked him.

He looked at me then. His eyes were red and he smiled like a clown from a circus, minus the face paint. I didn't know how anyone else in the Break Room hadn't noticed it.

"Only Jesus can protect us from the bong hits," he said wistfully.

He walked back past me towards the cart, grabbed a rag, and walked back in without my guidance. I hadn't even begun to show him the System of cleaning rooms. It was Mac's impatient air brought on by weed that fueled his actions. He walked over to a lampshade that was on a light above the nightstand in between the beds and dusted it.

"Only Jesus can protect us from the bong hits."

He then wiped the nightstand down with the rag.

"Oh Jesus, please protect us from the bong hits."

He turned it into a prayer as I watched. I grabbed my tray full of chemicals and shut the door. "You're nuts, dude."

I had known Mac since we were twelve. We went to different Elementary Schools, but every year our schools got together for a regional program for the gifted kids called Omnitrek. OmniTrek had different workshops for kids like acting, painting, or dissecting animals. The workshops lasted up to five days which meant it also took you away from the bullshit of learning the other mundane subjects with the rest of the regular class. The homework required for the regular classes did not apply to you if you left for OmniTrek. That was the best part.

During one of the OmniTrek workshops Mac had been placed in my group. We dissected a frog together with two other boys. It would be a year after that in middle school where Mac and I would have the same P.E. class, and I would see him every day for at least a year. Whereas the Mac I had known from OmniTrek was reserved and inquisitive, the Mac I would come to know a year later had changed drastically. He got horrible grades and was placed in the remedial classes. I don't know why this was but I never considered him stupid. I knew there was a spark of intelligence in him, hidden.

"What have you been up to, dude?" I wanted to catch up with him to see how he had been these last couple of months.

"Pretty good, man. Just smoking a lot of weed."

"Nice."

Mac had always been a bit overweight. He started smoking cigarettes when he was fourteen, stealing them from his mother who worked nights as a nurse.

It was a laborious, long day. I showed Mac how to clean the room according to the System. He said he understood but his inebriated state still had him attack the rooms with a slow randomness. I cleaned the first two rooms with him watching from afar. After I did so, I gave him the initiative.

"Hey Mac, I'm going to check up on some things at the Office. Keep cleaning this room and I'll be back in twenty minutes."

I walked out and down towards the Office but kept walking. I was on a search for Allan. I wanted to give Mac this time as a test to see how quickly he could get a single room done. Passing the pool I found Al with a Laundry Cart near a room on the west side. Walking up, I drew the curtains and shut the door.

"Hey." Al was gathering sheets off of a bed.

"Find anything?" I asked.

"Nah. Nothing good. How's Mac?"

"Stoned. I don't think he'll last here for more than a month."

He stopped. "Huh," he grunted like a young caveman eating a piece of meat, throwing the ball of laundry from the bed onto the floor and sitting down on the bare bed he had just stripped, turning on the TV.

"I've talked to Hel about working here. I'm thinking we'll get him here within a week or two."

"Sweet."

We watched TV and sat for another fifteen minutes before I felt the need to go back and check up on Mac.

"I better get back and see if he's even close to getting that room done."

I opened the curtains and prepared to leave. On cue Al got up and snatched up the remaining laundries returning to work. I returned to the same room Mac was in when I left. The beds, the trash, everything was undone. Walking into the bathroom I saw Mac on his knees, wiping the floor. He had tried to clean the mirror above the sink but streaks smeared the surface giving it a dirty look. Everything else looked wiped down and finished. It had taken him this long to get this far.

"How goes it?" I asked.

Mac stood up. He was out of breath.

"I'm going to my car for a second dude. I'll be back."

He dropped the rag and left the room. I picked up the rag, finished the floor, and started to work on the rest of the room. I took out the trash and both of the beds were done by the time he came back, with the smell of weed lingering on him stronger than ever.

<u>Tarney and Salad</u>

Mac Whiane lasted for three days at The Motel before he stopped coming into work. This created tension with Bonnie, as although the rest of us showed up to work every day to bust our asses, Mac was the first sign that maybe our selective employment pool of close friends should be more closely scrutinized. The day after Mac stopped showing up to work Al and I sat in his dining room eating dinner when his mother, who had cooked us lasagna and was smoking a Doral in the living room, brought the subject up to us.

"What about Mac?" Bonnie asked us. She still had her Motel Shenanigans apron on with the big familiar "M" on the front decked out in red.

"What about him?" Al replied in between spoonfuls of cheese and meat.

"Well, is he coming back or not?"

"I don't know. I don't think so," he said.

Bonnie paused to drag from her cigarette.

"Tell him we don't need him anymore."

It was already assumed he would not be coming back.

Bonnie's proclamation seemed wholly unnecessary as we knew we

wouldn't see Mac for another couple of months. He would most

likely be strung out in his basement on a couch, high or drunk.

"I was thinking about asking Ken Tarney to work with us," I

said to Bonnie.

"I really don't know," she said. "We don't want another one

of your friends walking off of the job."

"Oh, I wouldn't worry about that. Ken Tarney is a good

student in school that has never smoked a cigarette in his life. He's

Mormon and he goes to church every Sunday."

She seemed to consider this.

"Alright. I'll think about it."

I continued to eat my lasagna. I had met Ken around a year

before at a friend's birthday party. We had several reading classes

together. He hung out with Turtle on a regular basis, even though

they were extreme opposites. Ken was a devout Mormon who never

touched a single chemical in his lifetime. He didn't even drink cola.

He was also an avid skateboarder; his idea of a good time was going to the local mall and ride around for hours on a skateboard.

...

"I can't work on Sundays."

"I know that dude."

Ken, Troy Salad, Turtle, and I were in Ken's Blazer. We were headed off to the mall so that I could buy a Bob Marley CD.

"You want a job, Salad?" Salad and Turtle were both in the back of the Blazer, and Turtle spoke to Salad directly.

"Fuck yeah, man. I can dig money."

Troy Salad wore thick glasses and a Pantera Cowboys from Hell T-Shirt. He was a year younger than us but rivaled only Turtle when it came to the number of substances that he had ingested. Salad was hilarious. He smoked, drank, and treated everyone like a Brother.

We pulled up to the Mall of the West and walked in. We always chose a back path through a service entrance into the mall. The walls were naked of spackle and paint, bare drywall with patches of plaster to cover the naked screw heads, nothing else. Walking past empty plastic trash cans smudged on the insides with dirt and grime, we headed down the hall to the double doors that led into the mall itself. Through the narrow vertical windows we could see scores of people walking about in between the shops, mothers with children, teenagers on dates. We pushed open the doors and headed straight to the escalator where the Best CD's was. Ken tapped his fingers on the moving belt rail of the escalator when he asked Turtle and I,

"What would I being doing at the Motel?"

"Oh, the shit I've heard," Troy said.

"Yeah," Turtle said in agreement with Troy, without explaining himself.

"Rooms," I explained to Ken. "Cleaning, wiping, vacuuming. You find some crazy shit in the rooms sometimes."

"What have you all found before?"

"Packs of cigarettes, weed, porno, I've found anal beads in a room once. You keep what you find. Sometimes we find beer too," I beamed proudly.

"I'm not interested in any of that," Ken told us. "I could use the money though."

"Sure."

"I could use the money and anything else I could find," Salad broke in.

"I'll talk to Bonnie about it. She gave an OK to Ken working with us, but we'll have to see if she'll let you too. She isn't too happy with Mac Whiane walking off the way he did."

"He did?" Ken asked.

"Yeah."

No surprise registered on anyone's faces.

We got off of the escalator and headed into the Best CD's. Turtle had gotten me hooked on Bob Marley earlier in the year and I wanted to have a CD of my own to listen to. Ken and Troy wandered off to browse.

"Damn dude, I can't wait to get them started," Turtle said to me. "This is going to be so fucking cool."

I found a Legend compilation and brought it to the counter. As I was purchasing it Ken and Troy appeared.

"Find anything?" I addressed them.

"Yup," I said, holding up Legend.

"Let's go."

...

The day after I talked to both Ken and Troy about employment I walked into Al's house after school to discuss it with his mom. She was on the couch in her usual spot smoking and watching a Soap Opera. She had gone to work earlier and had just gotten back from the Motel not even two hours prior.

"How was work?" I asked her.

"Fine. I really look forward to the summer when you kids are out of school. Makes my day a heck of a lot easier."

"I can understand that." During the winter because of school Bonnie lost half of her workforce, at least during the weekdays. "I talked to both Ken Tarney and Troy Salad. They want a job at the Motel if you'll let them."

Bonnie laid her eyes on me. "You know Turtle came over here the other day. When I opened the door he was standing there and you could tell he was on something. His pupils were so big I thought they were going to pop out of his head."

"Wow. Really?" I knew of Turtle's habits but didn't think he would just come over to Allan and Bonnie's like that on drugs blatantly.

"These other two kids don't do drugs do they?"

"Oh, no. Ken Tarney for sure doesn't, he's religious. As for Troy Salad, I'm not sure, but whenever I see him he's sober."

Bonnie pondered this as she smoked.

"Tell them to be at work this Saturday so we can start training them."

I stood up to leave when Bonnie quickly addressed me again.

"Do you want to work nights after school working the Desk?"

"Sure. Yeah."

"This weekend when you come into work you'll shadow Roy. It'll be a one-day training. Then we'll set you up for work Monday through Friday after school, for six hour shifts."

"Alright."

"Do you still want to work in Housekeeping during the weekends?"

"Oh yeah."

"See you Saturday."

Saturday came and I walked into the Break Room. Ken Tarney and Troy Salad were there at the dirty table already, filling out their employment forms. Bonnie was at her desk filling out the charts; when she saw me come in she stood up and tossed a desk shirt to me (the desk shirts were a light blue, whereas the general housekeeping and maintenance shirts were an ugly tan.) I took off my shirt and put on the desk shirt in its stead. It felt nice to know I was going to be doing something other than cleaning after people. I wouldn't have to deal with anyone's bodily fluids, at least for a short while.

"I'll train you boys personally," Bonnie said to them. They finished up filling out their forms. Bonnie gave them the ugly tan long-sleeved Motel Shenanigans housekeeping uniforms and left me with Roy.

Desk Training

Roy attended to some faxes in the Office. When he was done he came into the Break Room. I had just donned on the desk clerk shirt and waited to be instructed. Roy lit a cigarette and stood there watching TV with me.

"Have you ever made coffee before?" he asked me.

"No."

"That'll be your first duty. You have to make coffee every morning for the customers." He walked over to the coffee pot on the shelf by the door leading out to the Lobby. He flipped the top, exposing an empty back chamber.

"You add water here. In this circular bowl," he pointed to an indented bowl in front of the empty chamber, "you put in a filter full of coffee grounds. We advertise free coffee in between 6am and 10am."

He took the cigarette from his lips, ashed it into an ashtray on the table, and put it back into his mouth.

"Come with me."

I followed him into the Office. The Office was a large room separated in the middle by a counter. On the other side of the counter was the Lobby. It had a tiled floor. Swinging glass doors led into the Lobby. By the door was a stand that had a small coffee pot. The coffee was made in the Break Room, but brought out here.

In the Office two touch-screen computers were situated on either side of the counter so that during busy times two clerks could handle customers. In the rear of the Office sat a smaller desk complete with a telephone and fax machine. Sporadically faxes would come through from the Motel Shenanigans reservation center containing the requests of different customers from across the nation that wanted to stay in our cheap luxuries. Leading out past the rear of the Office was a slender hall that led to a door to the Manager's apartment. The Motel Shenanigans always had an active manager that stayed on the Motel grounds whenever assistance was needed. Barbie resided there now. I followed Roy through the large Office and then into this hallway. Lining the walls of the narrow hall leading to the Manager's apartment were shelves of different lengths. The shelves contained towels, sheets, pens, paper, memo pads, and everything else an Office for a motel needed so that clerks didn't have to continually run in between the Office and Laundry

Room for supplies. Under one of the shelves on the floor was a large metal safe.

"You'll be collecting money from customers and then dropping the earnings in plastic bags into the top of the safe here." He pointed to a slit in the top of the safe.

"Will we have to ever open it?" I asked him.

"No. You'll never know the code. I don't either. Only the manager knows that."

Roy guided me back down the hall. He led me to a small grey metal cupboard hanging up on the wall by the entrance to the Office from the Break Room. I stood behind him as he opened it. It was full of keys.

"Every key that opens every door to the Motel are here in this cupboard." There were four sets each with different colored elastic bands on the ends, with four keys per set. They were divided into the colors yellow, red, blue, and green. "These are the Housekeeping keys. They only open certain sections of rooms. When Bonnie is making the Housekeeping charts, she hands out these keys to you guys so you can get into the rooms. Bonnie has to mix and match them depending on what rooms the Housekeepers are cleaning."

There was a mysterious set of uncolored keys with bland metal chains connected to the ends below the multicolored Housekeeping keys.

"What are these?"

"Those are the Master keys. They open every door in the whole Motel. Only the Maintenance Man and the Head Housekeeper would ever have access to these keys."

I made a mental note of that. I already knew that Allan had access to these keys for as long as I worked here, but now I knew where they were, and had an excuse to be in the Office area to have access to the keys for the duration of my shift. I needed to have a talk with him. We could make a copy of the Master keys and have complete access to the entire Motel at any time.

Unlimited Access to the Motel per Theft of the Master Key

After my first shift of training on the desk, Bonnie and Allan had taken me straight to their house for dinner. Bonnie made pasta with hominy as Al and I sat in his room downstairs. At the beginning of the winter Bonnie had given him the entire basement of their house as his room. He brought the environs of his room from the upstairs down to the basement, setting the TV against the wall and the futon and a wicker chair across from the Entertainment Center. The room was dark, open, and wide. The TV was playing that 80's horror movie Clownhouse, Al rested in his wicker seat and I was on his futon still in my dark blue Motel Shenanigans desk shirt when I brought up the most brilliant plan we've ever had in that god-damned place.

"I have unlimited access to the Motel Master Keys. I was thinking one of these days when I work the desk alone, you could take a Master Key to the nearest locksmith and make a copy."

"I already have dude."

His smile lit up like the Chesire Cat's in the dark.

"Why didn't you tell me?" I asked, shocked.

"I didn't want anyone to know, at least, for a while. I didn't want my mother to find out, as something like this could cost me my job. But around two months ago, I took one of the Master Keys with me on my lunch break on a day that I worked Maintenance and made a copy of it at the locksmith down the street."

I didn't know what to say. "Fuck yeah, man."

There was a knock on the upstairs door, followed by it swinging open. "Come get your pasta and hominy, guys."

We stood up to get our food. I watched that part on Clownhouse where those sadistic clowns were hanging one of the brothers from the tree in the front yard before I ran upstairs for dinner.

The Planned Kidnapping

I was working the desk after school on a Tuesday afternoon. I tended to what few faxes Roy had left me and was busy inputting customer data into our check-in computers by hand when a customer walked in. He was overweight and had a week's worth of stubble on his chin and cheeks. Besides the stubble he had a thick mustache under his nose and thick glasses to cover his eyes. He approached the desk.

"Got any rooms?"

"You know we do," I said with mild humor.

"How much?"

"Advertised as $44 a night but there is a $12 Nebraska tax."

"Damn."

He had taken his wallet out and was thumbing through what few bills he may or may not have had.

"That's a little steep isn't it?"

"What's steep?"

"The $12 tax. I've stayed in most of the surrounding states but I've never heard of a $12 tax."

"I don't know anything about taxes," I said politely. "I just know that after tax the price is $56.99 plus additional charges if more people are staying in the same room as you."

"Well…I can afford a room but my girlfriend is staying in the room with me. I can only afford the one person rate though…is that a problem?"

"Ahhh…no. Don't worry about it." I usually charged the regular rates, especially if it was a reservation placed over the phone. Right now I felt like being charitable since there wasn't a long line of weary travelers stretching out through the door who would all pull a mutiny on me at the front desk if I started cutting cheaper rates on some parties but not others.

"Oh, thanks man," he said. I took his driver's license from him and started creating his customer profile to assign him a room.

Patiently He walked over to the window of the Lobby across from the counter and stared wistfully outside. He was lost in thought and his eyes wandered to the supermarket to the west.

"You know I've been on the road for about two weeks now," he said. "I'm from Michigan and so is my girlfriend. We've been dating for three months. I met her in an online chat room and a month later she moved in with me. She has a one-year old baby and about a month ago the father of the child took the baby and drove off with it during a scheduled visitation. He fled with the baby down here to Omaha. I guess he's from here. My girlfriend hasn't seen her baby since. The plan is my girl and I are going to meet this guy in a public place, and then we're going to snatch the baby and run from him. He has no idea that I'm here with her."

My heart was beating fast. I didn't know if a call to the police would alleviate the situation in any way. What would I say to them, after he left? That a man told me he was going to kidnap his girlfriend's daughter from his girlfriend's boyfriend? This was the first time in my life where I was learning, as a seventeen-year-old boy, that sometimes nothing can be done to fix the problem. The problem wasn't mine to begin with. I wasn't going to get myself involved in the slightest. I hurried with my check-in process. I went through the name and his address in Michigan (which is the only part of the story I could prove to be true, as he had a Michigan driver's license.) I gave him one of the few non-smoking rooms we had left.

"That'll be $56.99."

He casually walked back to the counter, dug out three dirty wrinkled $20 bills, and handed them off to me.

"Thanks, young man."

"Anytime."

He walked out through the Lobby doors. I never saw him again.

From Housekeeping to Head Housekeeper

"You want to be the Head Housekeeper on the days that I have off, Joe?"

YES!

"You know I do," I replied, more coolly and professionally then the screaming voice in my head.

I had been at the Motel for six months. Winter was at its peak and several feet of snow lay on the ground. Bonnie sat at her cluttered desk, and now she was asking for me to carry the torch.

"We'll start you off with being the Head Housekeeper on the days that I have off. When the weather gets warmer we'll train you in Laundry too."

"Whatever you want me to do I'll do it."

Bonnie rarely had a day off, and when she did, Allan was usually the Head Housekeeper. He told me in secret that he didn't care for it all that much, as he preferred either Maintenance or Laundry. The Head Housekeeper made the charts in the morning for the other Housekeepers and checked on the rooms after they were done. This position also entailed slight disciplinary actions against Housekeepers if they missed something in a room. I wanted out of

Housekeeping and Desk. Being the Head Housekeeper was ideal for me. This would free up some time for me to hide away unnoticed from the majority of the others, to do whatever I wanted.

"I'll train you next weekend."

"Thanks, Bonnie." She leaned over and gave me my chart to work on. I stood up and threw on my flannel so I could hunt down Al and share the good news with him.

I walked out of the Break Room with the biting winter air hitting my skin. Al was working Laundry today. I walked into the Laundry Room and there he was, with a heat lamp on the folding table. A boom box blasted Westside Connection as he folded towels. I slammed the door.

"Your mom is making me Head Housekeeper."

"I know. She just told me last night."

"Awesome."

"I talked to her last night about putting Ragnarok here in the Laundry during the summer so I can do Maintenance. He'll start in April or May."

"Excellent. That's three of the major posts right there."

"There's something else."

"What?"

"Hel Samwig starts next weekend. My mother OK'd it."

There would be no need to hire anyone else. In between myself, Allan, Ragnarok, Turtle, Dickens, Ken, Salad, and now Hel, out of a Housekeeping crew of roughly no more than 18-20 people, we had taken over almost half of the cleaning compliment. During the school year we would run the place during the weekends, but during the summer we would control it every day. Also in possession of a Master Key, we couldn't be stopped. The Motel was ours for the taking.

"What about Turtle?" I asked Al. "Are there any positions open for desk?" I was plotting and scheming for the next big takeover of another major position, maybe another desk position, maybe a second Maintenance one.

"Fuck Turtle. You really think anyone else working here can work their way up like we have, Joe? No fucking way."

He had a point. Besides Allan, Ragnarok, and I, everyone else we had hired didn't work nearly as half as hard as we did. We goofed around and did all kinds of shit that would get us fired for sure, but we also worked hard, and knew how to work in most of the positions. Al knew how to run every post; I would be trained on Laundry as well to back up my Head Housekeeping position, and Ragnarok would be taught Laundry this summer. No one else showed such ambition.

"I guess it's for the best."

"Yeah."

I sat down in the dirty rag bin by the sink, my ass being slightly dampened from the juice of used rags. Al folded the towels for the upcoming day and we talked about the shit we would find in rooms and the sex we would listen to from total strangers.

The Flooded Laundry Room

"I wonder what would happen if I threw this rag into the drain behind the washer," Turtle said.

"Don't do it dude," Al warned.

Allan, Turtle and I were in the Laundry Room. I had worked every Saturday and Sunday for the last two months as the Head Housekeeper; winter was coming to an end, and the snows melted off the pavement into puddles on the sidewalk. Al was still in Laundry for now but in the upcoming weeks he was going to relinquish his role to work Maintenance, handing over the Laundry to Ragnarok. Al folded sheets using the torture device-looking apparatus, I was folding towels, and Turtle sat in the rag bin getting his ass damp. Turtle and I were usually the only ones to use the used rag bin as a seat because we didn't give a fuck. Turtle played with a dirty rag, twisting it in his fingers. It was covered in ashes from ashtrays. Small droplets of the Blue Chemical dripped off of the ends.

"You'd think the Motel would afford something as simple as a grate to put over the open-ass drain on the floor, of all things. I bet

I could fuck the whole drain up if I threw this shit in there," Turtle repeated.

"Yeah, but don't do it." Al wanted to rip this place off but in a more sophisticated style. He wanted to steal things. What he didn't want was for some reason to be held liable for something that went wrong in the Laundry Room, i.e. he didn't want to be suspected if something were to break or flood-out. He didn't want to get screwed over for Turtle's mistakes. Turtle threw the rag in between his legs into the pile underneath him. I finished folding some of the towels and grabbed my Head Housekeeping Master Chart.

"I have to go check some rooms for the desk."

"Yeah…I gotta go gather laundry from the carts so I can keep working." Al looked straight into Turtle's eyes. "Turtle; DO NOT THROW ANYTHING BEHIND THE WASHER."

"I'm not going to. I'm just going to gather up some sheets for my cart," he said innocently.

Al and I left Turtle in the Laundry Room; I headed for the Horseshoe. Al went in the opposite direction towards the South Side to start his rounds. An hour later I was on the Second Floor balcony inspecting rooms when Al ran up to me.

"Joe…you gotta see what that motherfucker did."

Turtle.

"What'd he do?" I asked.

"He did it."

"Fuck'n goddamnit;" I said. When the whole crew was facing a 10-14 hour day to get all of the rooms cleaned, a flooded Laundry Room was not what I was looking forward to.

I walked behind Al and lit up a Newport (courtesy of the skeletal fingers of Mrs. Long,) dragging gracefully from the tobacco and fiberglass mix. We took the closest stairs down to the bottom floor, which emptied us out by the Laundry Room. A stream of water gushed out of the Laundry Room and into the parking lot. Ragnarok, Turtle, and a handful of Mexicans stood there on the edge of the mini pond spewing from the room. I stepped into the water and looked into the Laundry Room; a plumber with a huge plumber's snake was twisting and cranking it into the pit that was the open-air drain. I looked back at Turtle as he laughed his chronic bronchitis 'I've been smoking since I was 14' laugh that didn't make any sound, but reddened his face. I glided over the water to where he stood.

"What'd you do motherfucker?" I said.

"Nothing man."

Al retreated into the Laundry Room next to the plumber. Barbie came out of her apartment to check up on the situation; she went into the Laundry Room too. The trio of Allan, Barbie, and the plumber by the drain went on for five minutes before Al came out to us.

"He just pulled out a rag from the drain. This is going to cost the Motel $3,000."

Turtle laughed even harder.

"Damn," Turtle wheezed. "What could have happened? Who could have done this?"

The Mexicans dispersed. I walked into the Laundry Room where Barbie and the plumber were. The plumber was hunched over. When he heard us he turned around and held up the same dirty rag that Turtle had been playing with earlier.

"You guys gotta be careful. If one single rag falls back into the drain like this, it could back up the whole sewage system."

The plumber unceremoniously placed the wet sopping rag on the table by the other towels. It dripped down on the table and off onto the floor in small droplets of chemicals and sewage. The plumber carefully put away his tools into a toolbox and walked out.

"We have to think of something to put over that drain," Barbie said. She retreated back to her apartment, leaving Allan and I in the wet Laundry Room.

Barbie Retires

"I'm leaving the company," Barbie muttered.

We were all in the Break Room eating lunch. Barbie sat at the table in between Turtle and Troy Salad. She smoked a cigarette. In between gulps of my sandwich I could taste her smoke.

"What?" Bonnie stopped eating at her desk and turned around.

"I'm leaving the company. Next week a woman named LaBelle will be coming in to head the Motel for a while."

We all took the news grimly. We liked Barbie and didn't want her to go. More importantly, she was mostly oblivious to the things us boys could get away with. A change in management might mean a change in routine, for better or for worse.

"Why?" Bonnie inquired.

"Oh, it's just about time." Barbie had been a great manager but to always be on call in all hours of the night had finally worn her down. We could hear it in her voice.

"We'll miss you Barb," Bonnie said.

We all nodded in agreement.

"Well, you kids have been a real good bunch," she said to us, taking a thick drag from her cigarette.

Turtle's Shit Fetish - Room 232

It was the end of March. I possessed a walkie-talkie and a thick key chain that had the keys to every room in the Motel, including some of the forbidden storage rooms. I was watching TV in the Break Room by myself and making adjustments to my Housekeeping chart when Turtle called out my name on the walkie-talkie.

"Joe, I need you in room 232. I repeat, I need you in room 232."

Turtle never used the walkie-talkie to call me from the Office to his rooms. I knew something wasn't right about this. I grabbed my keys and exited the room, turning a left and then another left into the Horseshoe. I went up a flight of stairs and reached 232 within five minutes of being summoned. Inside, Turtle was vacuuming the floor. The beds were all made, the surfaces wiped, the trash taken out. Troy Salad was on a bed watching TV. One of the laces to his sneakers was untied.

The room was dark, unnaturally dark for the light being on. I could only see a halo of light escaping the light fixture, permeating the upper walls. I looked up and saw that someone had taken a shit into the plastic bowl of the light fixture, and then screwed the light back into the ceiling with the light on. The heat from the light bulb cooked the shit to the plastic surface of the fixture. The smell hit me when my eyes adjusted to the brown mass above me.

"WHO THE FUCK DID THIS?" I yelled.

Salad didn't say anything. He smoked a cigarette, flicking his ashes on the floor. Turtle turned the vacuum off. He laughed the same way he had laughed when he had flooded out the Laundry Room. Instead of normal human laughter, small gasps of air escaped his teeth every five seconds, barely audible. His face was beat red.

"I took a shit in the light, Joe."

"Get it down and clean it out," I told him. "Make sure it's totally clean."

"Yes, Joe."

I walked out. My judgment got the better of me and I put my head back in through the open door to address Turtle with an ETA.

"I'll be back in five minutes. This better be done by then."

Staying true to my word I returned within five minutes to check on Turtle's progress. As I walked into 232 the smell still lingered. What upset me the most was the fact that we had to sell this room and the possibility of an innocent family being subjected to this stench was very real. I looked up at the light; the halo of light was gone, Turtle having cleaned it out. Straining my eyes, I could still see a black caked rim of shit that circled the fixture like the ring around a drain in a bathtub. The heat had cooked a ring of thin shit onto the fixture. Even I could tell that it was permanent.

"Goddamnit," I sighed aloud.

"Hey, we're sorry this happened," Salad said to me. He was standing now behind Turtle. "You want a chocolate to forget about all of this? We found an unopened snack tin in this room. You should have one."

My eyes flew down from the light fixture and into both Turtle's and Troy Salad's faces. Turtle had a metal circular tin in his hand; it was a chocolate tin, covered in a holiday motif. Santa Clauses and Snowmans adorned the tin. Already I sensed a trap, a gimmick. Something wasn't right. Turtle removed the top of the tin. Inside were chocolates and sugar cookies; on top of the sweets was a skinny dark shit that either Turtle or Salad had squatted and laid into the tin. There was also a burning smell.

"What the fuck...?" I breathed.

"I took a shit on it," Turtle explained. "Then Salad took some lighter fluid, dowsed it, and lit it on fire."

"Ugh," I said with a whiff of the burnt concoction they had made.

"We're going to offer some to the Mexicans," Salad said.

"You nasty motherfuckers," I sighed. "Go ahead. Just make sure to be back here in fifteen minutes to get back to cleaning rooms."

We all left the room together. Just as we did a Mexican by the name of Bernie passed the room. He was a really nice guy. On cue, Salad flagged him down.

"Hey Bernie! You want a chocolate?"

Bernie slowed down and stopped.

"Sure," he said with a slow drawl.

Turtle took off the top of the metal tin just as Bernie had his arm out, ready to snatch at the closest candy. Before he could touch the first chocolate, he saw the burnt shit lying on top like a brown dead worm. He withdrew his hand quickly as if it were a viper.

"They're delicious," Turtle proclaimed to Bernie in mock disgust. Salad and Turtle laughed together. Bernie shook his head violently and walked away. We went back to work.

Hel Samwig

The first time Hel had ever spoken to me was during the last portion of our Junior Year in high school. I was walking down Papio's hall when he saw me and pretended to roll up his sleeves to kick my ass. I knew who he was from Allan so I put a comical air into my movements, like Charlie Chaplin, turning briskly away from him so I wouldn't entertain his violent bullying actions. The minute that I did though, he snuck up and put his arm around me, and brought up his mouth to my ear as if we were lovers and he was going to nibble my ear.

"Don't you ever turn away from me again."

People walking down the hall around us parted like fish around a shark. Hel was six-foot-three (an inch taller than Allan,) and had a reputation for being crazy and out of control. His father was a drunk.

"Al was telling me about that nice little Motel of yours. I'm going to start working with you next weekend," he whispered into my ear as he let go of me.

I told him about Turtle and the shit he took into 232's light fixture. Hel stared at me like I was an oracle, a personal Jesus.

"Looks like I'm going to be at the right place then."

"See you next weekend. I'll personally train you myself."

Hel and the Laundry Chute

I trained Hel the weekend after I saw him. I was in the Break Room awaiting his arrival when he walked in through the door less than five minutes before 9 AM. He wore the grey long-sleeved shirt and big "M" patch on his left breast.

Bonnie and I watched the dirty fuzzy TV that was put into the cubicle above the refrigerator as Hel filled out his tax information. When he was done forty minutes later, I grabbed my chart and set of keys from Bonnie, nodding with my head towards the door. Hel stood up on cue and followed. Walking into the Laundry Room, I showed him everything. After the Laundry I showed him the Cart Rooms. We rounded off the end of the tour in the upstairs Cart Room. I closed the door save for a crack, as the light bulb to this Cart Room had broken off into the fixture years before, and nobody bothered to fix it. The only light available in this room was the light from the outside. I wanted some privacy with him, so I guided him into the middle of the room away from the partially opened door.

"You see this?" I pointed with one finger to the hastily made laundry chute cut into the floor. It was paneled on the outside by pressed wood, and the inside was made of corrugated tin. It was streaked black in different places.

"Wow." Hel's grin was huge; I was affirming to him that all of the stories that Al and I told him in school were true, and he was seeing it with his own eyes. The cheapness of everything sank in. From the battered carts to the dirty, dusty shelves, everything was making sense to him now. "This place is really fucking disgusting."

"I know."

I wheeled a cart out from the corner of the room and brought it in front of us, stocking the cart and showing Hel what we needed for our rooms. He stood there by my side obediently like a child learning his alphabet. I flung the door open and we pushed out into the cold, heading for our first room so that I could incorporate the System of Cleaning Rooms into his training.

In school Hel was a non-stop chatter box of sex and tits and vagina jokes and used his huge size and strength to bully his way into the personal bubble of anyone's comfort zones. He also jokingly alluded to homosexuality and pederasty, especially to smaller male friends who couldn't match his strength. This led to the hidden assumption spoken aloud by his peers that he might be capable of rape. These fears subsided after you got to know him and within weeks he was just another good friend, albeit a pervert. He was feared by those who didn't know him and loved by those who did. By my side now though, he was a mute and observant witness to the corporate world. He hadn't cracked one perverted joke in front of me yet, and actually looked kind of nervous as I trained him on his first job. I questioned him about it.

"Are you OK, man?"

He looked at me in confusion.

"What are you talking about?"

"Well...usually you're talking about raping us in a dark room or fucking a horse. You haven't said any weird shit yet."

A small smile spread out eagerly across his face.

"Did you want me to?"

I didn't know what kind of possible Pandora's Box I might have opened up.

"Well, just be yourself, man. You seem nervous."

He didn't say anything else immediately after that but it was apparent I had just taken the edge off of the situation for him.

The trash, the bathroom, the beds…I went through it all with him. He didn't show the initiative when it came to taking control of the room himself (he didn't assist me unless I told him blatantly to do it.) He stood and watched as I cleaned the room. Hopefully that was going to change soon. After three rooms, our laundry bag was full and he was still uncommitted to helping me in the slightest. Every other housekeeper that I had trained after the first room had at least helped with the trash, or taken the sheets off of the beds. Hel just stood there like my obedient parrot, watching intently and saying little. After the third room I was tired of this. I started to bark orders.

"Hey dude…I'm going to go downstairs to the Laundry to get more towels. I need you to dump the bag full of linens through the chute on the second floor so that Al can have more sheets to wash."

"OK."

I took my leave of absence from him. We did need towels for the rooms, this was true; but I also wanted my space from Hel, to see within twenty minutes if he actually would take the initiative by cleaning at least one room by himself.

I walked to the Laundry Room. Al was folding sheets and blasting Ice Cube. I shut the door and sat in the dirty rag bin. Before I sat, I used my hand to test the dampness of the topmost rags to see if I was going to soak my ass by sitting down. The rags weren't too terribly wet, so I sat down on them. Al walked over to the table by the rag bin and started folding towels.

"How's Hel doing?" He asked.

A load of laundry dropped from the second floor and down into the laundry bin in the corner. I brought my finger up to my lips; Al took that as a sign that Hel was just above us and could hear us through the chute.

We both watched the laundry drop. Then we heard something strange; it was the sound of a large thud. Something heavy was placed on the top of the laundry chute. Without another moment's hesitation, a sneaker appeared from the bottom of the chute, attached to a leg. Within seconds Hel dropped from the laundry chute into the dirty pile of linens below him. He fell on his ass, and stared at us with intimidating, bright eyes. His smile was as large as the sun.

We all screamed with laughter. The laundry chute wasn't an inclined slide that gently plopped you down into the bin below it; it was an open hole in the floor above us, and anything dropping from it went straight down twelve feet into the bin, pulled by gravity. Hel belonged with us after all in the Motel Shenanigans. He had just proved to us that he was a part of our team.

The Attempted Suicide – Room 121

School had just gotten out for the summer. All of us would now work every day, fully staffing the Motel. It was a Wednesday, and Bonnie had placed me in charge of the other Housekeepers. As a Head Housekeeper I headed off a staff of around a dozen people. Allan was placed back into Maintenance. Ragnarok had proved himself as the second leading best Housekeeper (second only to myself,) so Bonnie gave him the full responsibilities of the Laundry. Everyone else, Ken, Salad, Dickens, Turtle, and Hel, were all assigned as regular Housekeepers.

I had just pulled up to the Motel and walked in the door when Roy addressed me immediately. He stood by the door leading into the Office, smoking a cigarette. Al sat at Bonnie's desk going over charts showing which rooms in the smoking sections of the Motel needed bleach water rub downs to whiten the walls back to a sickly yellow instead of the dark brown-beige color of nicotine.

"The cops were here last night," Roy said. "There was an attempted suicide in 121. Some guy slashed up his wrists in the shower and got blood everywhere. After he cut himself up he called the cops and they showed up with five cruisers and an ambulance."

"Damn," I replied. Al showed no emotion.

"I want you to clean the room personally. I don't want any of the regular Housekeepers to clean up the blood, because of OSHA reasons. And be careful."

"No problem." In Barbie's absence Roy had become an informal interim manager. I could have told him I wasn't going to do it...but that meant someone else would. I accepted the task upon myself when Al stood up from the desk.

"I'll be waiting in the Laundry Room for you Joe."

Al left and headed for the Laundry. I went into the Office and printed out multiple charts, assigning them to all of the Housekeepers. Turtle, Dickens, Isabella, Jose, Ken, Salad, Hel, Bernie, Maria. I then went into the Office and pulled the appropriate keys from the key cabinet so that the Housekeepers could access the rooms. When I was done I left the charts and keys scattered around the Break Room table for the different Housekeepers. I then bolted from the room to find Al. The blood soaked room lingered on my mind and I wanted to see it as soon as possible.

Al was in the Laundry looking at a porno mag that was on top of the towel table. We kept a small cache of magazines behind the driers where no one checked. When I entered the room I didn't skip a beat.

"You ready?" I referred to 121.

"Yeah. Let's go."

I grabbed a laundry cart to drag along so that I could toss the soiled linens in. We entered the Horseshoe and within seconds were outside of 121. Allan took out his Maintenance keys and using the Master Key, unlocked the door. We entered.

Inside, it looked like a normal room. The beds were unused, the room clean. Looking around I saw that the trash can appeared to have torn pieces of paper inside of it. Other than that the room appeared untouched.

"It looks normal to me." Al inspected the walls for blood.

"The bathroom." I headed straight back for the bathroom. Al followed.

We entered the bathroom and immediately the copper smell of liquid blood faintly hit my nostrils. The walls in the bathroom, just like in the main room, were completely clean. Everything in the room was completely spotless. The shower door was closed, however; I stepped over and opened the door.

Blood streaked and dotted the walls and the floor of the shower. It hadn't thickened or hardened into coagulated droplets yet because of the water droplets also clinging to the shower walls. The man must have sliced his wrists while the water was running, washing most of his blood down the drain. The walls were painted pink with blood and soap scum. We stared at the blood for a good five minutes in silence before I reached over and turned on the shower, washing the remnants of the blood away. I grabbed the shower head and aimed it at every section of the shower wall so that I could get rid of it all. Al watched me with his arms folded across his chest. After I had finished, he spoke.

"I gotta get back to Laundry. Have fun with this shit."

He turned around and left the room. I surveyed the bathroom one more time; this would actually be a very quick room to clean since the only thing I had to worry about was the shower and the trash in the main room. The majority of the blood was gone now, so I was going to leave to get some disinfectant for the shower. As I walked through the main room and past the trash can, I decided to minimize my trip by taking the trash out with me. I pulled the plastic lining out of the trashcan itself. I noticed through the clear plastic lining that writing was on the torn paper at the bottom of the bag. Setting the bag down, I carefully inspected the inside of the bag for bodily fluids and needles (and finding none,) I separated the insides of the bag and picked out the contents of the shredded letter. I amassed the small pile of torn white notebook paper on the desk. It had been ripped up in such fine pieces that it was going to be a small task putting it all back together again.

I locked the door to 121 to give myself privacy in piecing together this man's possible suicide note, trying to first put together the note by looking at the front of the pieces of paper and trying to piece them together correctly based on sentence structure; this was not going to work. The sentences were written in barely legible cursive, and the blurred lettering confused me. Within moments of trying to piece together the note this way, I came up with a new plan of attack. I flipped all of the pieces over so that only their white unwritten sides were showing. There were about fifteen pieces total; I tried different combinations of pairing up the different ripped edges and when I found a match, I would keep those pieces together, and try the other pieces to see where they could fit.

After twenty minutes of working on the note, I had finally pieced it all together into one sheet. I left the note on the desk upside down and exited the room, running as fast as I could back to the Office and swiping a roll of scotch tape from the desk while Roy was checking in customers. I ran back to 121 and slid into the room, making sure a draft behind me wouldn't blow away the pieces of paper I had already assembled.

I stretched out and carefully tore off different lengths of tape from the tape dispenser, proceeding to tape it back together. When my task was done, and every rip was patched and taped up to their corresponding pieces, I flipped the letter over and was able to read the letter that this man had written before he slit his wrists.

"Dear McCloud Family;

I'm sorry for all of the trouble I have caused you with my drinking. You have spent so much time and effort on me, and I will always be grateful. Because of your efforts I had recovered from alcohol for a little while; I knew though that it would never last. I'm not going to put anyone else through what I've put you through. Yet again I love you so much and this will never happen again. I will see to it."

I picked it up gently and brought it to the Office where Roy was working, explaining what I had found in 121 to him and giving him the note. He quickly read it with little interest, but then went to the nearest phone and called the cops.

"Hey…one of our employees found a suicide note in one of the rooms…yeah, the earlier incident…yeah, that gentleman. He's in the hospital now? Good, good. Hold on to the letter? Yeah, will do…thirty minutes? It'll be here waiting for you."

Roy hung up the phone. I stood there gravely by the entrance to the Office from the Break Room and waited for any information.

"They're coming in thirty minutes," he said to me. "I'll give the letter to them then."

I nodded curtly and walked out the door, going back to 121 by myself. Once inside I drew the drapes and turned on the TV. I laid down on the bed trying to piece together what had happened in this room just the night before; I was holding a vigil for a man that had not died, but for his sanity, which most likely passed on during the night.

LaBelle

A month after Barbie ceded her managerial duties mid-summer her post had been filled by our new manager named LaBelle. LaBelle was an older woman of about fifty years old. Her stomach was huge, as if she had been pregnant once before and never stopped being that way. She smoked two packs of Camels a day. I could not imagine her ever being attractive. She had a mole or a growth on the inside of one of her eyelids. It festered like a small mushroom and was the size of a thimble.

We were all in the Break Room when she walked in from the Manager's Apartment and introduced herself. Al, Rag, Turtle, Dickens, Ken, Salad, Hel, and the rest of the Housekeepers were gathering their charts when LaBelle sauntered in, wearing a T-Shirt and sweat pants. Unlike Barbie who dressed somewhat formally with her blouses and dresses, LaBelle wore sweat pants that looked like she hadn't changed them in weeks and a T-Shirt. A Camel dangled from her lips as she addressed all of us together.

"My name is LaBelle and I will be your new supervisor. If you need help with anything let me know."

Bonnie smoked a Doral at her desk as she was completing the charts. "LaBelle is from Manhattan, Kansas. She just graduated from the Motel Shenanigans University."

"There's a 'Motel Shenanigans' University?" I asked.

"Sure is," LaBelle butted in. "It's not so much a University as it is just a hands-on training course. It lasts six weeks. They have their own state-of-the-art campus though, complete with shuttle system."

"Ha. Weird." I wasn't trying to be rude or arrogant so I dropped it at that but just the fact that the Motel Shenanigans had a 'University' opened my eyes. It made sense that they would need a Supervisor Training program, but to call it a 'University' made it seem like the Motel itself was the final resting ground for its graduates. No one ran the Motel Shenanigans. The Motel Shenanigans ran you.

A tall, goofy man holding a child walked in from the Manager's apartment through the Office and into the Break Room. He had a dirty 5 O'Clock shadow that was patchy and grey. His hair was a sickly brown and his Adam's Apple was huge.

"My name is Bob. I'm LaBelle's husband."

The baby, a large two-year-old wearing nothing but a shirt and a diaper, squirmed in Bob's arms.

"This is Peter," LaBelle started. "My no good daughter Sasha had him at 18 and then ran off to be a stripper. We haven't spoken to her in two years. She didn't even show up for the custody hearing. We're Peter's parents now."

Poor Peter. I had known this woman for fifteen minutes and already I knew his whole life story. Hopefully, and with both a little luck (and gumption,) Peter would find his way out of the archetypical White-trash upbringing he was thrown into.

LaBelle, Bob, and Peter retreated into the Manager's apartment. When they were out of earshot Bonnie was the first to chime in.

"They're something, aren't they?"

We grabbed our charts and headed out for work.

The Alabama Prostitute – Room 255

The first time I saw her she wore shorts that clung to her tiny ass, and a T-shirt without a bra. Her tits were tiny but perky. Her nipples poked at her shirt. She looked like shit. Her hair was stringy and straight. It thinned out prematurely. She was only in her thirties or forties but drugs had their toll on her already. I never knew her name. She was sexy. Dirty sexy. If I knew how to initiate sex with her I would have tried. In those simpler times though, there was no way I would have known how.

I walked with Allan and Ragnarok back from the Laundry Room and towards the Break Room when I saw LaBelle and the Prostitute from Alabama sitting on the cement curb in front of the Break Room door. Her T-shirt was loose and baggy, exposing her shoulders. Freckles littered her shoulders revealing a younger carefree existence of being in the sun often. LaBelle and Alabama were engaged in conversation.

"Yeah, I've lived up here myself for about only six months. There are differences in between Kansas and here," LaBelle said.

LaBelle was in the middle of telling her entire life story, the way we had heard it when we first met her. My eyes wandered from

Alabama's face and shoulders down to her legs. Her legs, like her shoulders, were covered in freckles. They were long and smooth. LaBelle took a pause from her life story to introduce us.

"This here is Allan, Ragnarok, and Joe. They've been working here at the Motel for the last year, going on two. Allan is Maintenance, Ragnarok is Laundry, and Joe here is the Head Housekeeper."

"Where are you from?" Al asked her. He sensed she wasn't from around Omaha.

"Alabama."

"What brings you up here?" I asked.

"I actually just left my husband. I have family here, but most likely I'll see them and keep on moving north."

She didn't seem like the LaBelle type to just jump in and spill her whole story in a matter of moments.

"What do you think of Omaha?" LaBelle asked her.

"I like it here. It's very...relaxed. Everyone is just laid back."

Alabama stood up and walked around the corner. LaBelle then told us everything about her.

"You boys keep an eye out for her. Her husband is a violent man, and he actually beat her when he found out she was selling herself for money. I told her we don't want her doing that stuff here, otherwise I'd call the cops. But if you see anyone suspicious walking around the Motel, let me know."

We went back to the Laundry Room to gather the Motel's dirty linen together. It certainly didn't take three boys to gather linens for the Laundry. It was a guise to keep us together so that we could reconnaissance information about Alabama.

We made our way around the corner from LaBelle's inspective eyes, heading straight for 128. Leaving the laundry cart outside of the room, we all took our respective seats around the room on the beds.

"Well, what do you think about her?" I asked.

"I dunno, man." Al's response.

Ragnarok gave his opinion. "I wouldn't. She could have AIDS or something."

"Yeah. You never know. I'll never fuck her but I bet she'd be fun if she'd let me," I said.

"Oh Joe, yuck! You never know where she's been. Plus she's old," Al replied.

"Dude, whatever. She's not that old. She's hot. If she'd let me I'd probably do it," I argued in defense.

An idea clicked in Al's head.

"What room is she staying in?"

"Why?" Ragnarok asked, confused.

"Is it a Connecting Room?"

Immediately the point drove home. Since I was the Head Housekeeper for the day, I could find out. I left the two of them in 128 and headed straight for the Office. I was going to find out what room she was in and hopefully, God provided, it would be a Connecting Room so that we could listen to her fuck.

Walking into the Office I went straight for the desk's computer, accessing different rooms and updating room statuses from dirty to clean for the sake of rentals. LaBelle was in the back of the Office at the Audit Desk. I was hoping to find LaBelle so that I could fish for information from her. Having her in the Office as I was accessing the computer was like hitting two birds with one stone. I could pretend to be working and updating the rooms right in front of her while I looked for Alabama's room.

"That southern woman, what room is she staying in?" I asked of her.

"255. Why?"

"Well, you never know. For her safety, if any of us sees a vehicle besides hers with plates from Alabama, or if we see anything out of the ordinary, it would be nice to know where she's at just so that we can report back to you."

"Good thinking, Joe."

My search on the computer was pointless after LaBelle effortlessly gave me that kind of information. I thought finding her room would be harder. On the computer however, I did find out that 255 was not a Connecting Room, so hearing her activities next door might be slim to nil. I knew Allan and Ragnarok though, and I knew that they'd still want to scope it out. I went back to 128 and knocked. After a bolt unlatched, the door opened up only a mere couple of inches. The chain was still fastened between the door and the frame.

"Yes?" Al's tan and brown face peered through the door and over the chain.

"255."

The chain instantly unlatched and we made our way up the stairs on the corner of the Horseshoe to reach 255. Hel's cart was parked by 233 and as we went past him he addressed us.

"Where you goin'?"

I answered him first.

"To 254. There's a hooker staying in 255 and we're going to listen to her."

Hel slammed 233 shut and followed us. The four of us reached 254 and, being as quiet as possible, entered the room. The room was Hel's room and was still dirty. The beds were tussled and covered with human body hair. A blacklight would reveal more if we had one. Picking up a glass and putting it to the wall, I listened through the end. Everyone else shook their heads at my desperation as they simply put their bare ears to the wall.

A moan. Or was it?

We stood there for twenty minutes, each of us listening for sex, for sighs, moans, groans, bangings, any sounds that might resemble Alabama getting fucked. I imagined her spent middle-aged body being assaulted by a random man that might have paid for her. Would it be a one-time fuck? Would he fall for her because of his loneliness, the same loneliness that drove him to her? Would he stick around for a couple of days, weeks, or months, buying her things like flowers and taking her out on dates, before she disappeared onto the next trick forever?

Nothing happened for those twenty minutes.

"We're not going to hear her. She's probably not even in there. I need to get back to work," Hel sadly lamented.

Ragnarok left next to gather Laundry from the Housekeepers. Only Allan and I were there last, with our ears plastered to the wall. Five minutes after Rag left we gave up too and went back to work.

Bonnie Gets Cancer

I slid the hominy into my mouth with my fork. Allan was at summer school taking electrical classes; he had failed too many classes during the last four years of his life and would not graduate on time. He took a full load of night school summer classes to compensate. It wasn't that he was stupid; nothing in school excited him or caught his attention. His grades and failures were a result of his lack of wanting to learn, and a bureaucracy that had grown so large that they didn't care. I was the one that helped him with his homework when he was home and plugged the numbers in his deficient schedule to help him graduate. When he wasn't there, I ate dinner at the house of my second mother waiting for him to get home in case he needed help with more school work.

She had let me in and sat me down at her kitchen table with plates for just the two of us. Even in Al's absence at school she set the table for me and treated me as if I were her own. We ate together talking about the Motel Shenanigans. We talked about the woman from Alabama at length, and Bonnie was even full of gossip concerning LaBelle.

"I guess LaBelle's husband Bob is fooling around with some young 18 year-old girl that is staying with them in the manager's apartment," she said.

"What?!?!?!"

"You haven't seen her?"

"No!"

"Some young girl that got kicked out of one of the rooms because she couldn't pay anymore. LaBelle took her in and I guess she even knows Bob is screwing around behind her back in the same apartment."

"Wow. Unbelievable," I declared in disbelief.

"I know."

Bonnie had finished half of her plate. She picked up her pack of Dorals and lit one. I chewed another mouthful of hominy.

"I have cancer."

I stopped chewing. The half soggy and undigested hominy sat in my mouth, empty and tasting like chalk. I forced it down my throat and set my fork down. I didn't say anything. I just sat at her table and stared at her, prompting her to finish.

"It's in my lungs. Doesn't really surprise me...I've been smoking for more than forty years. I started when I was fourteen. Pack a day since. The doctors tell me it's pretty bad, but who knows for sure."

She had made it to work on a semi-regular basis but now her prolonged absences, forcing me to be Head Housekeeper in her stead, started to make sense.

"Is that why you'll be gone for three or four days at a time during the week?"

"Yeah. I didn't want to alarm you or the boys but I've had to do chemo for the last six months. I tried to make it to work as often as I could but the chemo makes me dizzy. I can barely walk sometimes."

I loved Bonnie. Up until this moment for the last three years I was at her house four days on average out of a week. When Bonnie and Allan left for a vacation to Colorado last year, I was the only person they trusted to come over and feed their Beagle, Dolly. They hid their key underneath a cactus flowerpot on the porch for me.

Beside myself I finally spoke. "Does Al know?"

"Yes."

I wondered why he had never told me. He never kept secrets from me. The Master Key secret was the only other thing that he had kept from me. Cancer was a different matter altogether. Cancer was a big fucking deal.

Bonnie and I passed the time by making small talk about the Motel. An hour after I had learned that Bonnie had cancer Al came home.

"What's up," he said. I turned around to greet him as he passed by me and into his own kitchen. He made himself a plate of spaghetti and hominy and threw it into the microwave.

"I hate my teacher," he told us. "This guy is supposed to be teaching us about electrical codes and he spent thirty minutes talking about how he saw some guy getting gang-raped in his cell when he was in prison."

"Oh my God!" Bonnie exclaimed. "Why'd he talk about that?"

"I don't know. Some other guys were talking about their stints in jail and the Instructor just joined in."

"I thought this was a summer school class."

"Apparently it is, but it's also a Community College credit. The class is based through the local Community College. Papio lets its students take the class for credit as well."

Bonnie fumed. "Can you report him to anyone?"

"I can't. He told me he'd help me on my Final."

The microwave ringed. After two minutes Al's food was done. He grabbed it, nodded at me with his head towards the stairs, and took off down them. I followed. I looked back before I descended to see Bonnie staring off into space, puffing at her cigarette.

Downstairs Al turned on the TV and sat down in his wicker seat. I sat on his futon. He flipped it to Howard Stern and ate his noodles.

"How long did you know your mom had cancer?" I asked him.

Al slowly chewed his food.

"When she found out about it. Six months ago."

"Why didn't you tell me?"

He swallowed his food and looked at me.

"My mom has cancer Joe," he said stoically.

He resumed eating his food.

Turtle Finds His First Meth Rock in 105

Bonnie had a chemo appointment the week after I found out she had cancer. On the day she had to take off I was appointed as the Head Housekeeper. That Saturday morning I had finished gathering laundry. Turtle had a section of rooms right by the Laundry Room, so as I was walking by his cart, Walkie-Talkie in hand to report differences in room statuses to the front desk, Turtle stuck his head out of room 105.

"Hey Joe...you should come in here."

"What is it?"

"Just...get your ass in here man."

I walked into an otherwise already cleaned and excellent looking room; then I noticed it. On the nightstand in between both double beds, a small white rock was laying by the telephone. Small, white flakes surrounded it; it looked like anyone could have just shaved off a small part of it with a razor, or even a fingernail. Turtle didn't waste any time.

"I was cleaning this room when I found it. What should I do with it?"

"Flush it down the toilet."

He looked at me with a small grin on his face. As quickly as he grinned he turned around and picked up a rag, wiping dust off of a lampshade.

"I think its crack, man. I'm going to take it home and smoke it," he said.

"Turtle, take it and flush it down the toilet. Don't even mess with it."

"Ahh...alright."

I walked out of the room. The entire episode lasted for about five minutes. What I wouldn't know is that Turtle, once I had left, picked up the rock and slid it into his pack of cigarettes. This rock was to be his first meth rock, and would begin his lifetime addiction to methamphetamines. Within weeks he would experiment with the rock he had just found and smoke it all within less than 5 days. He has been hooked on meth ever since.

The Alabama Prostitute Revisited – Room 225

There is nothing to start your day at work other than to know that a violent breaking and entering had taken place the night before at your area of employment. Dickens, Tarney, and Salad were in the Break Room when I sauntered in. LaBelle sat at the table with them. They all seemed grim.

"You know Betty in 255?" The rest were silent as LaBelle spoke to me.

"Who?" I asked.

"That woman from Alabama you met about maybe a week, a week and a half ago."

"Oh. Ok. Yeah, what about her?"

"Her husband came up here looking for her last night. He actually had been searching for her for the last month or so. Well, he found her car and what room she was in and busted down her door looking for her. She called the cops, and the only thing that saved her life was the chain on the door. The frame to the door and the dead bolt are busted. Thank God the cops arrived in less than fifteen minutes. When he saw them coming into the parking lot with their lights on he fled downstairs, jumped into his truck, and drove off.

The whole door needs to be replaced."

"That's crazy."

The others gathered up their charts.

"Where is she now?"

"We've relocated her to room 225."

Pause. No way. 224 and 225 were the original Connecting

Rooms that I had heard my first sex act in, with Allan and Ragnarok.

I knew the chances of us hearing her fuck had just gone up

exponentially. I filed out with the others towards the Laundry

Room.

"Any of you want to go see room 255?"

"Sure," they all said at once.

They followed me like children following the Pied Piper.

When we got to the room the damage was apparent. The bottom of

the door had been kicked out in the corner; it still was intact, but it

didn't seal with the door frame any more, which was splintered and

fractured where the dead bolt used to be. Police tape covered the

door. I gently kicked the door further open so that we could see the

inside of the room. It was dark and the dead bolt was lying on the ground mere feet away from the door. Wood splinters littered the floor.

"I can't wait to tell Al and Ragnarok about this shit. Do you guys realize she's now in 225?"

All three of them looked up at me.

"So?" Salad responded.

"So, 224 and 225 are Connecting Rooms. We can hear everything that's going on in her room. We can listen to her fuck."

"Oh, shit!" Dickens said.

Tarney and Salad kept quiet. Ken Tarney wasn't the kind of guy you would drag into a room to hear other people having sex next door. He was devoutly religious and his plan was to save himself for marriage. His lack of enthusiasm was to be expected. Salad, on the other hand, was unexpectedly silent.

"What about you, Salad? You want to check on her room later?"

"Nah. It's nothing I haven't heard before." This surprised me. Salad was the type of guy that would stick his ass out of a car window and take a shit for the next car to see. To watch him have this type of mature reaction was unthinkable.

"Whatever. I'm going to get Al and Rag. Dick, you coming with me?"

"Sure."

We left the other two to gaze at the destruction that this angry husband had left behind in his wake. We made it to the Laundry Room where Al was reading a magazine.

"You want to go to 224? LaBelle moved that prostitute to 225."

He dropped the magazine down onto the folding table and joined us.

"Where's Ragnarok?" I asked.

"He left to go get laundry," he replied. "We shouldn't wait for him though. Let's just the three of us go together."

We tip-toed to 224, shut the door, drew the drapes, threw on the chain and bolt, and put our ears to the door connecting both rooms. Right away we heard the sounds of violent fucking. Slapping sounds were the only thing we could hear. No groans, no moans, no low whisperings of sweet nothings being barely audible. The only thing we could hear were the rhythmic pattering of flesh on flesh.

How coincidental and lucky we all had been. One, for Alabama to be moved into this room, and two, for us to be lucky enough to run right in and hear her already in the middle of being fucked. Ragnarok was missing out.

This continued for thirty minutes. The sound of either balls against thighs or her stomach against his continued until we heard our first moan as it escaped her lips. Another ten minutes passed; a second moan came from her, a long, drawn out moan, like she couldn't control herself anymore. It ended with a long, loud moan from the man, and then we knew it was over. Sitting down on the bed, Al put his finger to his lips. It was an unspoken rule for the Connecting Rooms to maintain silence for up to ten minutes before listening to see if the neighboring room had settled down enough to open our own door and glide out. After five minutes we could hear Alabama's door open and close; then there was dead silence.

"The coast is clear," Al whispered. We stood up and made our way out of the room. Al opened the door and walked out, followed by me, and then Dick. As I walked out and to the left in front of 225, I noticed that the door to 225 was cracked open, with the chain on the door. Through the cracked door I could see

Alabama on the bed wearing little except a T-shirt and boxers, with a pillow under her ass, and her legs spread out. She smoked a cigarette. Her eyes locked on mine. I did not avert my eyes from her, and instead drank her in from her head down. The trashy clothes, the propped up abdomen and legs slightly spread (she was in boxers but she still was probably doing this to air herself out.) As my eyes wandered back up to hers I could tell she knew. She knew what we had done; she knew that she had just been listened to for the entire duration of the last past hour. Her eyes were a mixture of confusion and embarrassment.

We walked away with her ass in the air to recover.

Crack and Meth – The Junkie in 106

There was a huge illegal immigrant deportation bust that happened in Omaha during the summer of 1998. Bonnie had told us that undercover cops working with the Mexican government had tracked down multiple illegal immigrants throughout not only Omaha but in the Midwest, sending them back to Mexico. We lost most of our Mexican Housekeepers during that summer. A few legal Mexicans remained. Our work force had been crippled and nearly cut in half. During the summer when everyone was traveling because of the nice weather, every motel in the nation was pretty much booked two weeks in advance. The disappearance of the Mexicans was heartfelt and somber. We all wanted them back. It was because of their disappearance that we were all forced to clean an average of 25 rooms a day. This would mean cleaning from 9am until possibly 9pm, depending on how fucked up the rooms were.

Because of her cancer Bonnie was placed on medical leave. Before the medical leave, her work days dwindled down to a couple of days a week. Finally mid-summer she had to leave indefinitely. She had lost twenty pounds, and began to lose her hair. By default I was to be the primary Head Housekeeper.

One summer evening in 1998, less than a year before we would all graduate high school, the Housekeepers were given thirty rooms to clean, each. It was roughly 7pm at night. I spent that day checking rooms for the desk and tidying up the imperfections that my peers had overlooked. An ashtray full of ashes here, a missing Bible there. I walked by 106 with my large metal keychain dangling from my side. A young man called out to me from the doorway.

"Psst."

I stopped. "Yes?"

"I need a phone for this room. Mine doesn't work. Can you help me?"

"Yes sir. I can do that. I'll be back with a new phone in fifteen minutes."

"When you come back, come back alone," he said ominously.

My blood pressure elevated, like a rabbit in front of a wolf. What did he say? The door shut as quickly as it had opened. I stood there, confused. What should I do?

My curiosity overrode my judgment. I went up to the Maintenance Room for a new phone. The Maintenance Room was above the pool room on the second floor. It was a fuck-all mess of

nuts, bolts, screws, tools, and plumbing snakes thrown onto a work

bench that hugged the wall. There was a small skinny aisle that led

its way against the opposite wall. The room suffocated me. Three

phones not quite brand new but in working condition sat on the

bench in no particular order. I picked one of them up; the side of the

phone was covered in cigarette burns. I picked up another; it was

(looked) fine. I made my way out with my bounty and shut the door

behind me.

Should I get Al? Rag? LaBelle? Why should I walk into

this strange man's room by myself, especially if he suggested I do

so? I felt a sense of commitment to customer satisfaction if I didn't

get there as soon as possible. What if this strange man was an

honest person that needed a phone? I hesitantly went back to 106,

knocking on the door. My heart raced. What was going to happen?

The same man answered. He was in his mid-twenties, had a light

complexion, and was ghostly pale.

"Come in."

The phone swung in my hand as I lumbered into the room.

My defenses were up and my heart raced. The strange man went into the bathroom. I followed him slowly until I reached the night stand between the beds, taking a sharp left. I untangled the phone on top of the night stand. My judgment kicked in and before I fully disconnected the old phone, I picked up the receiver and put it to my ear. Dial tone. The phone worked. He lied to me.

I quickly disconnected the phone and put the new phone in as a replacement, wrapping the cord of the old phone around my fist and then wrapping the rest of it around the phone itself, so that if this weird man came lunging out of the bathroom, I would have a makeshift weapon that wouldn't leave my hand. Facing the bathroom (and not turning my back on it,) I slowly paced backwards to the front of the room to leave. I was five steps away from turning around, opening the door, and bolting when the bathroom door opened and his voice wafted through like a bad smell.

"Come in here."

I should have run.

I didn't.

I slowly inched myself towards the bathroom door. Across from the door was a mirror on the bedroom wall. It was body length. Instead of giving up all of my chances for escape and blindly walking into a trap, I looked into the mirror. My left foot pointed in the direction of the front door in case I needed to flee. When I looked into the mirror all my worries melted away. My hand relaxed on the grip of the phone as I walked into the bathroom.

The man was bent over the sink. He had a baby food jar in his hand and inhaled white smoke coming out of it using a straw poked through the lid. On the sink were six or seven baby food jars, each with a hole in their lids, and a straw through each hole. Some of the jars had a yellow rock in them, some of them had a white rock, and yet some of them had a white powder. Each of their respective jars had either a white or yellow coating on the side of the glass. This man wasn't a rapist or murderer. He was your out-of-town traveling typical drug fiend. Thanks to Turtle I was familiar with his type. At ease I stared at the multiple jars set before me. The strange man spoke.

"This one here is crack," (pointing to the yellow rock,) "and this one here is meth," (pointing to the white rock.) "I also have Angel Dust if you want any. How old are you?"

"Seventeen."

"How long have you been working here?"

"Going on two years."

"Well hey…if you or anyone else wants to party here tonight, I'm going to try to get some girls to come. You want to smoke any of this shit with me?"

"Ah, no man. To be honest I've only smoked weed until now and I don't want to change that."

"That's fine. Just remember what I told you. Come back here later tonight after work and I'll hook you and your friends up phat."

"Thanks," I said amused.

My inhibitions gone, I turned and slowly walked out the door. In the Break Room, Turtle and Allan both sat at the table. Turtle smoked a Newport and Al watched TV. Because of Bonnie's cancer (and leave of absence from work,) Turtle gave us rides to and from the Motel.

"I'm done with all of my shit. You guys want to get going?" I asked.

"Yeah," they both said.

"Turtle, you got a cigarette?"

He flipped a Newport in my direction. I remained silent about the junkie; I knew that if Turtle knew about him, he would be at the Motel all night partying.

Room Full Of Pillows – Room 119

"I have a special assignment for both of you."

Allan and I sat at the table in the Break Room with LaBelle and Bob.

"We're getting more than a hundred new pillows for the Motel. I need both of you to help unload the pillows and put them in 119," LaBelle told us.

We followed LaBelle and Bob out of the Break Room and down the sidewalk into the Horseshoe. At the east end of the Horseshoe was a van. LaBelle, Al, and I gazed at the van while Bob fiddled with the lock. After he got it unlocked, he flung the door open and behold! The van was stacked floor to ceiling with hundreds of pillows.

"What you can't fit into 119, just stuff into this storage room here." She pointed to a small room without a number to the left of 119. We very rarely ventured into that room. It was half-full of phone books.

After LaBelle and Bob left us, Al took his shirt off in the hot summer sun and started throwing pillows at me. I caught his pillows and then tossed them in no particular direction into 119.

"God I love this place." Allan was lost in awe.

"Let's arrange these pillows and put them against the back wall."

"Gotcha."

We closed the door to the room and carried the pillows to the back, lining them up and stacking them neatly on top of each other. Initially appearances deceived; the mound of unorganized pillows by the door barely covered the entire back wall when organized. We still had a whole room to fill. Going back outside, the cycle repeated itself for three hours; unload, toss, throw, carry, organize. By the end only the bathroom was free of pillows. The whole main room was packed, stacked, and stuffed. You couldn't see over them or through them. The entryway was partially clear and large enough so that two people could stand in the room and shut the door, only to face a wall of fluffy pillows.

I bolted the door. Al dived head first into the pillows. With a small running leap I jumped on top; I fell backwards slightly, so I had to try again. I jumped as far as I could and had to use my hands to pull myself up to the top. When I got there, there was no sign of Allan.

"Al?"

Muffled laughter beneath me.

I dug into the top layer of pillows and sure enough, Al was almost right under me. He had burrowed himself into the middle of the room and had been under me the whole time. He pulled himself up and out of his burrow and laid back on the top of the pillows. I crawled to the TV and dug out the screen so that we could see it, flipping it on. Merlin with Sam Neill was playing. I stretched out on the top of the pillows by Al and we watched TV. It was then I thought of Bonnie.

"How's your mom?"

"She's OK. She stopped smoking and she takes chemo once a week. I had to pay rent this month because she's broke."

"Damn."

"Yeah. I'm kind of angry at her. I've been telling her to quit smoking for years and she just didn't listen."

The thought of Al paying rent while still in high school saddened me. The boy had become a man.

"I wonder how long Turtle is going to live," I said, my thoughts wandering from Life to Death. He had been a regular smoker for the last three years.

"I'd place a bet on 40. He won't live past that age. If it isn't the cigarettes that'll kill him, it'll probably be some kind of other drug."

"40? Hard to say. I'd say 50 years old. Sure enough he won't grow up to be an old man."

Turtle had experimented and smoked that white rock that I told him to toss into the trash weeks before. He finished it off in less than a week. He first tried smoking it in a regular glass weed pipe thinking it was crack, but it melted to the consistency of water and dripped down the pipe, burning his mouth. After learning that the rock was crystal meth, a friend of his had shown him how to freebase using foil. Ever since then Turtle had been asking everyone for meth connections. His habit was no small secret and we all knew about it.

"He doesn't care if he lives or dies," Al commented.

"I know. With him though, it's anything for the adventure, eh?" I said.

"You hear that Whore upstairs fucking again?" He asked me, changing the subject.

"Not since the last time with you."

"Something weird is going on upstairs," he said. "There's a bunch of women staying in rooms 217 through 224. I went to try to listen to Alabama again but 224 was occupied by three or four girls. I saw them entering the room; they were wearing nighties and pajamas and shit. In broad daylight. LaBelle thinks that they're a prostitution ring; they traveled up here from Louisiana on a big red bus."

"Why does LaBelle think they're prostitutes?" I asked.

"She told me that different customers staying upstairs at night will be walking around and these girls will walk up to them and ask them if they want sex for money. I guess a family on vacation to Yosemite had been staying upstairs, but got a refund after the dad of the family was walking along the balcony and was propositioned by one of them. He gathered up his family, complained to LaBelle, and left after LaBelle refunded him in full."

"How many rooms do they have?"

"I don't know but I think it's around a dozen or so. And in each room, there's four or sometimes even five girls sleeping there."

"That's fucked up."

"Rag and I will be walking downstairs in the Horseshoe when we'll see a half-dozen girls sunbathing on the cement. Most of them do it without their tops on with their tits hanging out."

"WHAT!" My excitement had peaked. "Dude, if you see them doing that come get me."

"Oh, for sure."

An idea went off in my head.

"Hey…we should make this room we're in a main Cache room. Like 215. I wouldn't mind having a beer right now on top of these pillows watching Merlin throwing lightning bolts at people."

He nodded in approval. "That's a great idea. Actually that works the best because all of our other caches are in rooms that can be or are rented out to people. By making this a Cache room, no one will find it."

An eventful day. It was decided that 119 would now be the base of operations for our Hidden Caches, although 215 would still serve a role. And as for the young prostitutes wandering the grounds at night begging for sex…I couldn't wait to meet one.

The Prostitution Ring – Rooms 217 through 224

The prostitutes had exactly seven rooms lumped together. Their red bus was a huge old rusty thing, hulking in the parking lot by the entrance; it was too big and cumbersome to navigate into the Horseshoe. Their rooms were on the second floor balcony in the inside of the Horseshoe, secluding them from the entrance to the Motel but giving them an eagle's eye view of all of the rooms in the Horseshoe itself.

I was walking with Al when I first saw them. We were collecting laundry together and turning around the corner towards the Pillow Room of 119. As soon as we were in the Horseshoe I saw three girls, young women of no more than 25, all of them wearing bikini bottoms, and none of them wearing tops. However, they were sunbathing and lying on their stomachs, only exposing the nakedness of their backs. We stopped at our first room to collect laundry, sequestering ourselves from the outside world.

"Did you see that?" Al commented.

"Holy shit yeah."

"Who in the hell just sunbathes at a place like this half-naked?"

"Prostitutes," I said bluntly.

"Good point."

We collected the laundry and left the confines of the room to seek Ragnarok. He would love to see half-naked girls with us. Rag was in the Laundry. We pushed the cart into the sanctuary of our home base and told him what we saw.

"Rag," Al said, "there's some half-naked prostitutes sunbathing in the Horseshoe right now."

"Let's walk by 'em," he said.

The three of us went out and down towards 119. When we got there, they were gone.

...

The next day I was cleaning the pool with the Motel Shenanigans' net. It was an ancient thing, still blue like the day it was made, although tinged with brown from the bacteria and mold that feasted on it. Small bits of leaves clung to the mesh net, also to be dispelled when they decomposed entirely.

Allan and Ragnarok walked up to me from the Break Room. They entered the pool area through the cheap painted brass gate and stood before me.

"They asked us to fuck them last night," Al said to me.

"What the hell are you talking about?"

"He's right," Rag confirmed.

"After you left work yesterday Joe, Rag and I came here to go swimming. Before we could jump in, five girls walked up to the gate and they asked us to talk to them. We went over there and they were all like, 'How old are you?' 'Have you ever had sex before?' 'If you want to hang out with us, let us know. Me and my friends here are staying in 220.'"

"Rag, what did you do?" I asked.

Al spoke up for him. "Nothing."

"Nothing?" I said.

"Yeah, nothing. Rag didn't say a word the whole time."

I laughed.

"So what did you do then?" I pressed.

"We just kind of stood there talking to them for a while. You should have seen what they were wearing, Joe. They wore nothing but silk lingerie with no panties. You could see their asses and bush if their movements were timed right."

"That's so weird." You'd think whoring yourself would be more of a discrete activity. Sure, you don't want to be dressed up for an Amish holiday, but to give yourself away that easily? It didn't make sense to me from a business point of view. By doing that, you'd receive the wrong kind of attention, not just from possible Johns, but from the law.

"They went back to 220 after talking to us for a while. We swam for about an hour before we took off too."

I gazed out past the cheap gate up to 220. Nobody was out walking around. I wondered what was happening behind those closed doors.

...

The prostitutes were expelled a week later.

After prancing around the Motel at night with their nighties and inquiring for sex, a couple of our respectable customers called the police. Enough reports had been submitted for the police to start taking action. The police called LaBelle to warn her that they were going to arrest anyone soliciting sex at the Motel later that week, and that they would set up their own undercover officers as Johns to catch them. Whether it was an act of being a good Samaritan or not wanting a police presence on the premises, LaBelle cancelled the prostitutes' reservations for the block of rooms they were staying in and gave them 48 hours to leave.

We saw them leave. I pulled up with Al in his white hatchback (he had just gotten his license.) As we approached we saw LaBelle outside, defiant, standing her ground, back and shoulders erect. The prostitutes were dragging their luggage and packing their shit into their big red bus. A slim, black girl of nineteen years old wore nothing but a silk red nightie. I could see the bottoms of the cheeks of her ass. She eyed me and Al both. Even when they were being dispelled they were on the hunt for male weakness. She was gorgeous.

"And why do we have to go?" The matron of the prostitutes had presented herself, an older fifty-year-old woman with a grey beehive hairdo. She looked like a Sunday school teacher, wearing a conservative plain flower-patterned dress. She was the only one of them with a voice.

"Because we don't want your type of business here." LaBelle said.

"What business?"

"You know what kind."

"No, I don't."

"Look, we can refuse service to anyone. Get out of here."

"I know what it is," the matron said with a broad sweep of her arm, "it's because I have an interracial family. I didn't think I could get treated like this in today's day and age."

I swept my eyes on the band of women before me. There was not one man present, and yes, there was a good mix of all races present, all dressed in lingerie and not wearing shoes. They were a family; this could not be disputed.

The angry matron and her sexual daughters jumped on the bus and the matron herself got behind the wheel. With a clunk, the engine started, and they roared off into the morning. From the Laundry Room Ragnarok and Hel had seen the whole thing; Al and I stood behind LaBelle as she smoked. I was full of questions. I needed answers.

"Why'd you do it, LaBelle?"

"The cops called me and told me they were going to start arresting them. We can't have that kind of business here."

'Did you do it to save them?' I thought without speaking.

Inadvertently she had. By kicking them out now they could wander

to the next motel and set-up their business again. If she really

wanted to stop it, she would have gotten the cops involved. I turned

around with Al to go to the Break Room. Dickens, Ken, and Salad

looked out from the doorway. They had seen the whole thing too.

The Car Salesman in 237

"You know that stuff is still going to kill you." I said it with nothing but love for Bonnie.

"But this is an herbal blend. It's not real tobacco." She was immediately defensive.

Bonnie had gotten bored of sitting around the house and wanted to be productive again. Her hair had fallen out in patches due to the Chemo. She had gotten a wig from the cancer society and wore it everywhere. It looked fake, and one could tell that the wig was made from real human hair. Whose hair it was, and how old it was, was a mystery.

She was back as the Head Housekeeper for three days out of a week and today Bonnie had come to work. She placed me into Housekeeping. I was given a chart with 16 rooms on it, all rooms on the second floor, on the inside of the Horseshoe. Bonnie gave me the list as she took a puff off of an herbal cigarette.

"It doesn't matter," I continued. "The smoke is what causes cancer. You could work in a burning tire yard for thirty years and not smoke tobacco, chances are you'll pick up something there too."

She immediately extinguished the cigarette in a nearby ashtray.

"Well shoot."

I appreciated that she did that for me. I didn't want her to be sick. If she could prevent any further sickness I was all for it. Grabbing the chart from her I went upstairs, entering 235 and 236 and cleaning them without any problems. After these two rooms I made my way to 237. It was a Stay-Over; that is to say, there was a customer in the room on extended stay, but we still had to clean the room and make the bed. We were not allowed to touch any personal belongings or affects that the customer may have left in the room itself; to do so much as look into luggage or move things around was punishable by a Write-Up, which was a negative written report placed into your file. Stealing from the customer was punishable by termination, and legal action would also be faced.

I knocked on 237.

"Hello? Housekeeping."

No response. I carefully opened the door. No one was inside. I walked into the room when the smell of shit hit me. My nostrils flared. The smell was like a suggestive and vague waft that floated through the entire room. My eyes scanned my surroundings for the source of the smell; to my left on the desk next to the TV I found it immediately. On the desk a dozen Styrofoam cups were placed carefully apart from each other. The tops were covered with plastic wrap that was attached to each cup midway down the side with a thick rubber band. I looked down into the cup closest to me and saw a stool sample. My eyes adjusted in the dim light. As I moved away from the cups I noticed dates had been scribbled on the side of each cup with a pen. My eyes wandered to the TV; on top of it there was a small dirty toupee. It looked like a rat that had lost half of its body. Ignoring the faint shit smell I walked into the bathroom. The smell still permeated the whole room and the bathroom even as I put distance in between myself and the cups full of shit. I looked into the bathroom and saw an enema bag draped over the side of the shower; the bag itself was on the outside of the shower, while the ever-so-long tube and nozzle protruding out of the bag were slung over the wall of the shower like an obscene proboscis. The tube and nozzle were on the inside of the shower, with the end of the nozzle pointing down towards the drain.

I ran out of the bathroom and called the Laundry Room for Allan. When Bonnie was back at work Al was usually given Laundry privileges while Ragnarok was forced back into Housekeeping like everyone else.

"Please," I thought to myself. "Please be in the Laundry Room."

Two rings. He might be on the grounds somewhere, gathering laundry from carts.

Third ring. Allan answered.

"Hello?"

"Al. 237. Get your ass up here. You have to see this."

"I'll be up in a minute."

I closed the door, save for a small crack so that Al could let himself in. I went back to the shit cups and looked into each one. None of them were solid samples; they were all a smooth brown paste, each one a sickly brown or black color. Something was wrong with this guy. I didn't know if he was saving his own feces as some kind of sexual fetish or if he needed to document and record the different dates of his bowel movements for medical purposes.

Ten minutes later Al walked into the room. Immediately I could see he sensed the smell. With urgency I walked behind him and shut the door, locking and latching the entire thing just in case Bonnie or the proprietor to the room arrived.

"Look at this."

He followed me as I hovered over the shit cups. He noticed the contents and the dates on the sides.

"What the fuck...? Wow." He couldn't say much more than that.

"Follow me," I said.

I led him into the bathroom and with one shaky finger as if I was the Ghost of Christmas Future, I pointed to the enema bag. He stood in front of the shower, staring at the bag and the tube and nozzle through the wall of the translucent soap scum shower wall.

"Let's go through his other things," he said.

"Great idea."

Outside of the bathroom door against the wall was a luggage stand. It was small and black, and could collapse to provide more space in the room. On this luggage rack was a big dark suitcase. It was zipped shut. Al unzipped it and opened it. A leather bondage suit was in the luggage. A matching black leather mask, with zippers on the eyes and mouth, stared up at us like a grisly golem sleeping until it needed to be awakened again.

Al picked up the mask and fingered it lightly.

"This guy is a fucking nut," he said.

"I know, I know."

"What do you think the shit is for?" he said.

"I don't know. At first I thought it was for medical reasons. After seeing this shit in his luggage though, he's gotta be doing it because he's a weird deviant or something."

He set down the mask and carefully rummaged through the luggage. On the side hidden by a blue shirt was a three foot long black dildo. Al used the shirt in the luggage to pick up the dildo by the base. He held it at arm's length. It had a huge black head that was out of proportion with the rest of it, and it was ringed with several tiers of thick plastic that looped around it on the way down. A fake black imitation vein vertically covered the shaft. With every arm movement, Al would cause the big black penis to shake. After around twenty seconds he put the dildo back into the luggage.

"Either this guy's a deviant, or he's got a sex life that no one can imagine."

We inspected other portions of the room. I went over to the nightstand and opened the drawer. A pager was sitting on top of the Gideon's Bible. Two black film canisters were in the drawer by the Bible as well. I took the first one out and inspected it. A roll of film was inside.

"I wonder what's on these," I said.

He came over to where I was and I handed him the film canister. I took out the second canister and opened it. It was full of marijuana.

"This guy smokes weed."

Al gave back the first canister and I gingerly put it into the drawer. After inspecting the weed he put the canister down on the top of the nightstand, but with the lid off of it.

"You have any small plastic bags on your cart?" He said to me.

"Yeah, I do. I have a roll of bags for the ice buckets." I already knew what he had in mind. "You're not going to steal his weed from him, are you?"

"Of course I am. What the fuck is he going to do, call the cops on us? 'Officer, a housekeeper at my hotel stole my weed?' He can't even complain to LaBelle. She'd laugh at him."

He went over to the door to get a small plastic ice bag. I moved some other knick-knacks in the drawer around when I noticed a small white medical bracelet. I picked it out and read it.

"Our mystery man here has a name."

"What is it?"

"Hermes Sniper."

He digested that mentally.

"What a fucking weirdo."

He opened the door and looked right to left. No one in sight. He quickly grabbed a small ice bag from my cart and shut the door, relocking it with the bolt and chain, and brushed past me straight for the weed on the nightstand. He dumped half of the weed in his baggy.

"That's kind of fucked up, you know," I said.

"He won't need it. And I'm not taking it all, just half. And look at it," he said as he held the bag aloft, "it's all shake. This stuff is garbage."

He finished up his thievery chore as I walked over to the shit cups again to stare. The medical bracelet was still in my hand. He was obviously some kind of sexual deviant, but was it a mere coincidence that he was also sick and needed to save his stool samples? As Al pocketed the weed and unchained the door to leave, I picked up the rotten old toupee on top of the TV, and placed it on my head.

"Al," I called out to him.

He opened the door and looked back.

"I'm Davy Crockett!" I said with a southern accent.

Al laughed at me. "That's so fucking disgusting, dude. That thing could have lice or something."

I put the toupee back on the TV.

"I'll be down in the Laundry Room. Call me the next time you find something like this again," Al said.

He turned and left. I put the bracelet back into the drawer, picked up a rag, and started the chore of finally cleaning this man's room an hour after I had walked in.

LaBelle Retires – Enter Brody Charmin

"I'm transferring back to Manhattan, Kansas."

We were all in the Break Room when she told us. Bonnie was at her desk. She wasn't surprised by it. She already knew.

"Why are you leaving, LaBelle?" I asked her.

"I just miss home. That's all."

It was the end of the summer of 1998 and within a year and a half we had lost two managers; first Barbie, and now LaBelle. I heard a man's voice (different from Roy's) in the Office and I looked past LaBelle to see a man sitting at a desk in the back. He had beady cold eyes and a thinning hairline.

"Your new manager is here. His name is Brody Charmin. He just graduated at the top of his class from the Motel Shenanigans University."

Great.

On cue the man with the beady eyes came into the room. He lit a cigarette.

"My name is Brody. Nice to meet all of you."

He was missing portions of his left arm. I tried to be discrete, narrowing my eyes for a few seconds to see what was wrong with his arm. His underarm above the left wrist was gone. A thick chunk of his meat had been removed halfway up to his bicep.

A woman materialized from somewhere in the Office. If Brody was in his forties, this woman looked as if she was in her late sixties. Her hair was nasty and unwashed. It clumped together in different spots. She was freckled, and possibly the most unattractive woman I had ever seen. She had to be a Tweaker. She looked as if meth was in her daily diet.

"Nicetomeetyou," she barked. It was said so fast I could barely pull it apart. Her voice was masculine. She sounded like she had scraped her vocal cords with sand paper.

"I'm a no-nonsense guy," Brody commented. "If you all stay on task though, there's nothing to worry about."

"Youwantsomecoffeedear?" The woman asked Brody.

"No thanks hun," he replied.

She turned the corner and went back into the Office.

"Yup, that's my wife. I had a wife before her but she couldn't keep her legs shut. She might not be a looker but Marsha will never cheat on me."

Bonnie gasped. I heard someone choke on their coffee.

Silence pervaded. Brody left the room.

"I'm on One" – Mad Drawings from the Acid Lunatic in 146

Ragnarok and I were in the Laundry Room folding towels for our carts when Allan came in, out of breath. He pushed a laundry cart into the room and heaved it towards the wall.

"You guys gotta see this."

We followed him to room 146. 146 was by the exit to the parking lot of the Motel, right by the pool. He opened the door and immediately Rag and I were astounded.

Every single inch of wall had been written on or colored in with a black, permanent marker. Like some fucked up art exhibit, we slowly made our way around the entire periphery of the room taking our time to soak in the details. "I'm on One" was scribbled repeatedly, over and over, on all four walls. By the twin beds, a light fixture was secured to the wall with two lamps attached, one for each bed. On the left lampshade, "I'm on One" was written in huge block letters. On the right lampshade, the phrase "A bed time story – Once Apoun a Rock Winnie the Pooh Snamped." (*sic.*) Underneath the right lampshade and above the bed, the words "Trust Nobody" was written. The word "Nobody" had a long devilish tail on the letter "y," and a tombstone sprang out of the letters "bod."

"What do you think it all means?" Ragnarok asked, to no one in particular.

"I know what it means," Allan beamed.

"How could you know what all of this shit means?" I asked him.

"Well," he replied, "when I first came in I was just like you. I walked in, saw all of this shit, and thought to myself, 'this is going to take forever to prime and repaint!' I saw the 'I'm on One' over and over and didn't know what the hell that meant. As I was leaving the truth was written on the bottom of the door."

We went over to the door. Rag and I studied it for the Truth. On the peephole, whoever had stayed the night before had drawn a man bending over with his pants down – the peephole was his asshole. Below this, a huge caricature of a man with well-defined abs covered the whole bottom half of the door. His pants were unzipped and his large, grotesque penis limply hung down to his knees. The caricature had the face of a gargoyle. He wore a sideways cap, and next to him on the left was the phrase "Fucking dope Hoe$ hop on this big dick" (*sic*) and to the right, "$uck my dick if you don't like my shit cuz I waz on One when I did this – I took Asid" (*sic.*)

Ragnarok and I read at the same speed apparently; when I reached the "I took Asid" part I started laughing, and so did he. Whoever had decided to stay the night before in 146 had made the conscious decision to lock himself/herself away from the world and drop LSD. They must have also decided that they would need nothing more than LSD, privacy, and a black marker to pass the time.

"This is insane," I remarked.

"Yeah, it is kinda funny that whoever did this left that last comment on the door near the bottom so you couldn't see it."

The "I took Asid" remark was very small and could have been easily missed. I imagined the planning phases from the long-haired cracked-out hippie that did this beforehand. All he needed was LSD, a marker, and a Visa card.

"We have to show this to everybody," I said.

Al and Rag left the room but kept the door cracked open for reentry. I hunted down Turtle and Ken. After gathering both of them with the same cryptic message ("Man, you gotta see what this crazy asshole did to this room!") the three of us made our way to 146.

We wandered around the room. Independently we all took a corner of the room to ourselves to view the scribbles that the madman had written on the wall. I saw something new with each glance. On the bathroom door, the word "Bathroom" was written. The two O's in "room" were drawn like eyes, and a mouth full of teeth was below that. "Stay out for about 15 to 30 min."

"Have you ever done Acid, Joe?" Turtle asked me.

"You know, I haven't." I replied.

Ken had never done a single drug in his life. His upbringing was against it. He was raised to monitor his caffeine intake from little to none at all, let alone dropping LSD or smoking marijuana.

"Turtle, I don't know how you do this stuff. I'm glad I'm clean," Ken said.

"Yeah well, life's not an adventure unless you try new things, especially those things that can break down the ego and make you one with God," Turtle said philosophically.

"You don't have to do LSD or any drug to believe in God," Ken said. "God actually wants you to be clean and sober to experience true happiness."

"On top of that," I said to Turtle, "I thought you didn't believe in God." I was mentally referencing the multiple times that Turtle had ranted about the negative impact of organized religion and how self-destructive religion could be.

"Oh, I don't believe in a lot of things," Turtle defended himself. "I don't believe in Jesus, or Mohammed, or any other status symbol of what God is supposed to be. In fact, Jesus himself would be pretty ashamed of the human race if he knew that people still carry on with their actions and sins, and do it in his name. The Crusades, the Inquisition…Jesus would have never wanted to be a part of those things. Human beings have inherent flaws but they try to cover them up in God's name to justify themselves.

"The first time I did LSD," he continued, "a lot more happened then just the visuals and hallucinations everyone talks about. I was broken down. I can see why some people commit suicide after taking it, or are crazy for the rest of their lives. You lose everything within yourself, and you want it to stop. Hours into it you realize though that you and your whole life has been nothing, but that you have also been everything, and linked to forces that no one can control. I don't know about a God or gods, but I know that there has to be something out there."

"But God wants us to be in contact with Him. That's why he sends the prophets." Ken's religious upbringing was really coming out now. I inwardly groaned. "Joseph Smith. Over time God does what he can for all of his children. After Jesus' death, God sent him to the Americas to continue preaching. People forget the Word and Message of God, and since he wants to be active in our lives, he sends prophets from time to time so we can't forget. That's why God revealed the nature of Heaven again to Joseph Smith."

Turtle was not a vindictive person. Arguing with Ken would have been pointless. He would never change his mind. I realized my mind set was exactly like Turtle's. Turtle wasn't ignorant. This whole time I had thought he was an atheist, but never did I imagine he could be agnostic. I wouldn't be able to say anything else in the conversation now because I knew Ken would just keep rambling about the Mormon church. My disagreement with the Mormon faith is like that of any other faith; they claim to be the only one true

Faith. This isn't true. How can one Faith be above another?

Troy Salad walked in. "Ragnarok told me you guys were in

here…" he stopped abruptly at the sight of the walls. "Jesus."

Turtle and I laughed together at Salad's surprise and

mentioning of Jesus' name when we had spent the better half of the

last fifteen minutes trying to uncover the truth about God and

religion. In silence we wandered the room, absorbing the lessons

written by a madman's hand.

The Beginning of the End

"Dickens just called. He quit."

I was the first to hear the news. After a year and a half of steady employment, Dickens left us. I sat at the Break Room table stirring my coffee when Bonnie told me what Dickens had done.

"Does Al know?"

"Not yet. He's out on the floor gathering laundry."

I walked out to pursue Allan. This was pretty important shit. I found him pushing a cart on the second floor.

"Dickens quit," I told him.

"What?"

"Yeah. He just called and told your mom he's not coming back."

"Fuck."

"I know."

I opened a door to a room and we went in together. We sat on different twin beds and watched television.

"I bet he just woke up this morning and decided to get high, instead of coming to work," he mused.

"I'm thinkin' you're entirely right on that one." Dickens had been getting stoned almost every day for the last 6 months. After doing it for so long, maybe the Stoner Doldrums took control.

"Look at us," Al said aloud. "Me and you have been here going on three years. Whenever Dickens had a job before here he was there for maybe a couple of weeks or months before throwing in the towel. I'm surprised he made it as long as he did, but still."

"You want to find the others to see if they know?" I asked him.

"Yeah. Let's head back to the Break Room."

On the way back before we could even get to the door, Turtle, Salad, Ken, and Hel all walked out together with their Housekeeping charts.

"You guys hear about Dick?" Al asked.

"Yup. Bonnie told us," Turtle said.

"Just another day of cleaning rooms for those of us lucky to be here, eh?" I said to everyone.

We filed into the Laundry Room to get started.

. . .

The next day Turtle and Salad quit. The same scenario that happened before with Dickens played out. Turtle called the Motel ten minutes before our shifts began to tell Bonnie the news.

"I'm not coming in today. I quit. Salad is quitting too."

"Well, shit. Thanks for telling me. Don't put me down as a reference. The least you could have done is let me know weeks in advance."

"Sorry Bonnie."

Bonnie hung up the phone without another word.

When the remainder of our crew came into work, Bonnie filled us in on the developments. Ken Tarney showed up fifteen minutes late. We assumed he had quit too. While Ragnarok, Hel, Al, and I stocked our carts to prepare for the day, we saw Ken pull up in his Blazer.

"Look at that," I nodded to Al.

"I wonder why he's late."

A thought hit me. "It's no surprise if you think about it that Turtle and Troy Salad quit the day after Dickens did. What do you think they did last night?"

"Got fucked up."

"Right. They probably even stayed at the same place, partying it up with Dickens in celebration of his retirement. Most likely they woke up on the floor of Dickens' room, looked at each other, and decided they would quit too."

"I'll have to talk to Dickens about that," Al said.

Five minutes after entering the Break Room Ken Tarney emerged and came over to us outside of the Laundry Room.

"Hey, I put my two weeks in today. In the summer after we graduate I'm going to Italy to be a Missionary for two years."

"Dammit Ken." I paused. "Did you hear about Turtle and Salad?" I asked him.

"Ah…yeah actually, I hung out with both of them for a little bit at Turtle's house last night. They were going to go to Dickens' to smoke pot. I went home after they left. We all talked about quitting though."

"Do you know why they did it?"

"They're tired of having 20 rooms a day and cleaning up after total strangers. That, and I guess they just wanted to party for a week. Turtle spent his last paycheck all on meth and he's going to be awake for a couple of days. Salad is going to be driving around with him."

After a pause I questioned Ken. "Why exactly are you quitting?"

"I'm going to Italy."

"Yeah, you're going to Italy in a couple of months. No, I mean why are you really quitting, right now?"

Ken thought for a moment.

"I don't really like it here. I'm tired of cleaning up vomit. It's not sanitary."

Ken couldn't appreciate the perks of the Motel Shenanigans, I realized. Finding booze, drugs, cigarettes, and porn in rooms left over from tenants were not even factors in his equation. His religion prevented it. As for the more important aspect of the Motel Shenanigans, the memories, the stories, these were not good enough for him either. Finding dildos in rooms and listening to people fuck were things that a normal God-fearing Mormon didn't do. Ken Tarney was no exception.

"It was good working with you Ken."

"Likewise. Thanks, dude."

He ducked into the Cart Room and pulled out a cart. In two weeks he wouldn't be doing that anymore.

The Pound of Weed in 240

A week later everyone had 18 rooms to clean since half of our crew quit. As the Head Housekeeper I wanted to go home before 6pm at night, so I assisted anyone that I could to get done. I first helped a Mexican woman that had a whole block of trashed rooms, changing the sheets and making the beds for her. She was grateful. Then I checked up on Ragnarok, who was in 240. He was behind schedule, too. I went to ask him if he needed any help.

"Of course," he agreed. "Any help is welcome. I've had a fuckload of dirty rooms today."

"Have you seen Bonnie lately?" I asked.

"Nope. I heard she lost all of her hair though."

"Yeah." The chemo had poisoned her skin and blood to try to fight the cancer cells and keep them from spreading. She was losing her battle with Cancer.

When I walked in Ragnarok had already cleaned the majority of the room. The last thing he needed to do was make the bed. I carefully picked up the blanket and comforter and put them on top of the chair by the window, making sure not to unwrap them and let them drag on the floor. Ragnarok stripped the sheets and dumped them in his laundry bag.

"Have you seen Turtle lately?" Rag asked me.

"No," I said. "Have you?"

"No."

After fitting new sheets to the bed, Rag and I took the top and bottom of the blanket and fitted it to the bed. The coup de grace of finishing a Motel Shenanigans bed was to fit the comforter on top of the blanket and tuck in the corners.

Most of the comforters were thin, worn, and smelly. I was unsure of how long they had been on those beds. Like the blankets, they were washed twice a year (unless they were covered in shit or piss.) Every comforter was as thin as a piece of paper, and smelt like sweat. Being careful not to let the comforter spill out from his arms, Rag tossed me the bottom. The middle was still crumpled up.

"I wonder how long Turtle is going to live?" I said.

"It's hard to say," Rag responded. "It could be until he is thirty or forty. Most meth addicts don't live past fifty."

Rag and I stretched out the comforter to place it snugly on the bed. The middle opened up and unfolded like a parachute, bouncing up in the air. A pound of weed flew out of the middle and landed at my feet.

"SHIT!" I screamed. I ran and slammed the door shut, closing the curtains.

Ragnarok walked slowly around the bed to see what had jumped out at me. He treated it as if it was a live rattlesnake.

"FUCK DUDE, LOOK AT ALL THIS WEED!" I shook with excitement.

"Wow." Ragnarok was impressed by the bundle, but he wasn't as excited as I was. I became a cat covered in cat nip. I picked up the pound; it was not an 1/8th, it was not a ¼, it was not an ounce. It was a full fucking pound. The bag was sealed on all sides as if someone had carefully burnt the cellophane wrapping around the weed, and then pinched the melted plastic shut with their fingers. Either that, or they used some other device to wrap and seal it, like a meat-cutter's wrapping table, the kind that has a heated tray that melts and seals the bottom of the wrapped plastic to contain the meat within. I ran to the phone, calling the Laundry looking for Allan.

"Come on, come on…"

No response.

"Keep this here and out of sight," I said.

"Ok."

I ran out of the door looking for Al as fast as I could, running across the top balcony of the Motel like a hawk hunting chickens. No yellow laundry cart. That's what I was looking for as I ran down the stairs to the Break Room. Nobody was in there.

"Fuck," I muttered to myself desperately, "where the fuck are you?"

An idea clicked in my head. He usually had a Walkie-Talkie on him at all times. I ran into the Office. Brody Charmin was at the desk.

"Yes?" He said quizzically. My urgency alarmed him.

"Where's the Office Walkie-Talkie?"

"Right here." He handed it to me. "What's wrong?"

"Nothing. I just need to contact Allan."

Brody grunted and then turned his head back to his paperwork. Walkie-Talkie in hand, I left the Office and Break Room. The minute I was past the Break Room window I sprinted to the Laundry Room.

"Al?" I called out through the Walkie. "Al?"

"Yes?"

"Where are you?"

"I'm in 120 reading porn."

"Meet me up in 240 as soon as possible."

I ran back to 240. Ragnarok kept his promise. The weed was out of sight.

"Did you find him?" He said.

"Yeah. He should be here any minute…"

Al walked into the room. I slammed the door and locked it.

"What are you two dumb fucks doing in here all by yourselves?" He said.

"Where is it?" I asked Rag.

"Here," he said. He opened the drawer to the nightstand and pulled out the pound of weed.

"Holy fuck." Al went over and snatched the weed from Rag.

"How are we going to get this home?"

I looked at the bag thoroughly. The marijuana itself was green and brown. Buds and small leaves abounded. It was packed and looked like it was ready to explode out of the bag.

"What about using one of our hidden caches?" I proposed.

"No. We can handle a customer finding the booze or porn if they pulled back the bureau. We have so many rooms where we're hiding shit now, losing one room's treasure is no big loss. A pound of weed doesn't happen every day. I'll have to smuggle this into my house today, without my mom knowing."

The three of us stood in silence trying to figure out a plan. Finally, a plan developed in my mind.

"Al, do you remember that carton of cigarettes I found last week?"

"Yeah. Why?"

I was cleaning room 130 when I found an entire carton of cigarettes. Only one pack had been taken from it. I had taken the carton and threw it into our usual hiding place where our hidden treasures went, under the bureau in the main room.

"Listen. Find a way to bring the pound back to your house. Hide it in the trunk of your car. I'll get the carton of smokes and throw them into your car as well. We'll take them back to your place and we can hollow out the cigarettes with a toothpick. Then, we can stuff the empty smokes with weed, and tie off the end like a joint."

"That works. I'll take this shit with me now."

He took a pillowcase off of one of the pillows and put the pound inside of it. After this he opened the door and pushed the pillowcase down deep into the laundry cart, under all of the other soiled linens. He pushed away towards the Laundry Room where he could take the pillowcase to his car to hide our precious cargo.

I went to 130 after I checked my Head Housekeeping chart to see if it was occupied. It wasn't. I pulled out the bureau and there they were. The carton of smokes, a generic brand I had never heard of before, lay underneath. Pulling it out I walked to Al's car; I arrived just as he was hiding the pound of weed underneath his spare tire, in the wheel well. I handed the carton over to him and he threw it in next to the weed. He placed the spare tire back in its place.

"Come home with me tonight. We'll watch a movie or something, and pack all of the cigarettes that we can with this shit."

"Done deal."

He returned back to the Laundry Room and I went back to inspecting rooms.

. . .

When the day had finished I jumped into Al's car and we rode back to his house together. Luckily for us his mom left for the Casino and wouldn't be back until later that night. We had six or more hours to complete our deed.

Al threw <u>Phantasm</u> into his VCR and we sat and watched the Tall Man and his spheres while we unloaded the cigarettes. It was a two man job we had realized, and it was a good thing I had come along. I was responsible for emptying out the tobacco into a plastic grocery sack and putting the empty cigarettes into a pile on a small metal tin-plate so that Al could pack them full of weed.

We didn't smoke weed regularly and we didn't know how to roll our own joints. Although we both smoked cigarettes on occasion, a whole carton would last us a year. The idea was to use the paper as a pre-rolled joint, stuff in the weed, twist off the end, and then rip off the filter and twist that end shut as well. Fifteen cigarettes into the operation, I realized we couldn't possibly roll every single cigarette into a joint. The work was slow. Stuffing the weed was the harder job out of the two; the weed would poke and break the paper around it.

"How's it goin?" He asked me.

"Fine. I say we roll about forty joints and call it a night."

"Works for me. I can sell the rest of the weed in bags, and sell the joints for $5 or $10 a piece to junior high kids," he affirmed.

It took us about an hour and a half. By the end of the movie we had our forty joints. Al placed the joints in a sandwich bag and we put the remaining weed and smokes away in a cubby hole above the boiler in his laundry room.

"You want to smoke one?" He asked.

It was an unspoken clause of our toil that we had to. We both knew when we set aside the night for our task that we were going to have to smoke and try this strange weed that I found.

"Yeah. I'll walk home before your mom gets back."

He whipped out one of our joints.

"Let's go into the garage."

I followed him out to the garage. After snuggly shutting the door to make sure weed smoke didn't waft into the house, he lit the end with a match. He hit deeply and then passed the joint to me.

"You know I haven't touched this shit in three years," I said.

"This is my first time."

I inhaled the joint. The smoke was difficult to process. This didn't taste like the stuff I had smoked three years ago. Already a confusing mix of calming waves and paranoia hit me intensely. We had only smoked half of the joint. I couldn't smoke anymore.

"I'm done."

"What? You pussy."

He smoked the rest to himself as I watched. His mother had an ashtray full of butts down in the garage on the work bench in the back. She had a bunch of gardening tools on the bench next to her ashtray. The butts in the tray looked like they had been there for a while. Al took the last hit off of the joint and then put it out into the ashtray. He made sure that the remains of the joint were buried in ash, not exposing anything weed-related in case his mother was to use the ashtray again. We then went back into the house.

I couldn't walk straight. In retrospect I believe that the weed was laced with something, like PCP. I can never claim that I have smoked PCP, as I don't know what it feels like and don't want to know. The only thing that I am sure of is that the weed we smoked that night didn't feel right. Al agrees with me to this day.

We sat down and tried watching night time TV. The floor and the walls started retracting and I felt like I was going to be sick. My head was swimming. The world was spinning. It was like this for fifteen minutes before it cleared up enough for me to think and function, but I still felt somewhat sick. The nausea subsided with time. We became giddy and watched Howard Stern for an hour. By the end of the hour the giddiness was replaced with paranoia, a paranoia so intense I couldn't handle it.

"If this doesn't wear off soon I'm going to tell someone dude."

"What the fuck? Don't get me in trouble with this shit! Do you want something to eat?"

"Not really," I replied. "Actually I could use something small, like an orange or something."

"Let's go upstairs."

He shut off the TV. Upstairs in his kitchen he dug out two oranges from the crisper in the refrigerator and gave one of them to me. He peeled his with a kitchen knife. He seemed to be in better physical and mental health than I was. I tried peeling the orange but the orange slipped out of my hands and into the sink. Al laughed at me.

"You OK there, Joe?"

"I feel fucked up. But dude, I've been high before. It never felt like this."

"It'll be OK. I'm sure by tomorrow you'll be fine."

I clumsily picked the orange back up and tried to grasp it. The skin was wet and it rolled across the kitchen counter.

"HAHAHA! What the hell is wrong with you?" Al laughed.

On the third attempt of peeling the orange I was more successful. I held the orange in my hands and broke the skin with my fingernails. When I did this a stream of citric acid shot into my left eye.

"OW!" I painfully caressed my eye with the back of my hand, being careful not to use my citric acid soaked fingers on the eye itself. Al laughed his way into the living room and turned on Pulp Fiction. The part where Ving Rhames is being raped by a Hillbilly was on. I staggered to the couch and devoured my orange.

"I can't concentrate," I said. "I'm so stoned. Al, how are you feeling?"

"I'm stoned too."

"This doesn't feel right though."

"I have a dizzying feeling myself," he said. "Is weed always like this?"

"I don't think so," I said. "I'm never touching this batch again."

We watched Bruce Willis chop up a dude with a sword.

"I can't wait to sell this to people," he said.

"You can keep the profits," I replied. "I don't want to be caught up selling this stuff."

We finished the movie. At 11 O'Clock at night I walked home through La Vista, past Central Park and the creek where I used to catch frogs.

Bonnie Falls

"It looks good."

"Thanks. You can still kind of tell. Lord knows I feel the difference."

Bonnie had been absent from work during most of the winter of '98 because of cancer treatment. She had talked Brody into getting her back into work. I could see why; she was stagnant. She wanted her life back; she needed her mind preoccupied with her former routines. She wanted not just to feel, but to know, that she was still productive and useful.

She had lost all of her hair to chemo, bald now as a baby, save for wisps of sick grey hair sprouting in tufts around her crown. She was wearing the wig that had been donated to her. The wig was made from live people and sewn into a large elegant tuft. It would have been comical on anyone else if it hadn't been worn by Bonnie.

"This thing is so god damn itchy," she said to me. "It's hot, too."

We were the only ones sitting in the Break Room. Brody Charmin was in the Office at his desk.

"It's good to have you back, Bonnie." I knew of the dizzy spells that she had been facing for the last couple of months. I was surprised she had come back; most of the time when I went over to their house now, Bonnie was in bed, unable to move. To summon the strength to get out of bed and drive a car to work after all she had been through seemed like a miracle.

"Yeah well, hopefully it's for good this time. I can't sit around anymore. Rent money is running out."

The other housekeepers had already left to begin their shift. With Bonnie back, I was just another housekeeper. I got up and poured some black coffee into a small Styrofoam cup to begin my day.

Bonnie rose from her chair and went into the bathroom, shutting the door. I sat back down in my chair, going over my housekeeping chart.

THUMP.

A loud muffled THUMP resonated from the bathroom. Loud, because it was loud and very audible; muffled, because it wasn't a clean sound, but instead sounded like a stack of sheets or a bag full of rags had been dropped from the top of a shelf down to the ground. There was no other word to describe it other than a THUMP. It wasn't a Crash or a Bang, those pointed and precise sounds that happen when air meticulously shoots out in all directions within seconds to assail the ears, no, this was a soft and sullen sound, trying to hide itself, but couldn't. I sprang up. In my mind's eye I already knew what had happened. My heart raced. I walked over to the bathroom door and turned the knob. Slowly, I opened it. It stopped within inches of Bonnie's torso.

Bonnie had fallen. Her eyes were wide open, staring at the ceiling. She was on her back; a vacant expression resided in her eyes. She either had the wind knocked out of her or she was too proud to come to her senses and ask for help off of the ground. It could have been a little bit of both.

"BONNIE!" I yelled. Brody stood up from his desk in alarm. I carefully opened the door as far as I could and slunk into the bathroom.

"Bonnie?"

She didn't talk. She merely stared at the ceiling. Like a leopard I leapt down to my feet and slid my hands under her shoulders. I picked her up from the ground. When her body was elevated from the stomach up she tried to regain composure. She still didn't speak but her arm swung out and went around my head for support, as if some basic survival function was getting her through this. With her arm draped around my shoulders and my left arm providing support around her back and under her armpits, I stood up slowly, bringing Bonnie to her feet. Her legs buckled under her. She hung like a limp fish on me. Forcibly I stood up at full posture, opening the door and dragging her to her desk. I placed her gently back into her seat. She was out of breath. Absentmindedly her hand flicked out and tried to grab her pack of Dorals that she usually had by the side of her ashtray. The cigarettes weren't there of course; she had given them up to try to save her life, but now it might be too late. She laid back against the chair and regained herself. Brody stood in the doorway.

"Is everything OK?"

Bonnie didn't respond.

Brody stared at Bonnie. His left arm twitched against the wall, the missing mass from it visibly showing what little muscle he had left. It pulsated like a heart. After assessing the situation, he turned around and headed back to his desk. I sat down at the table and lovingly gazed at Bonnie.

"Are you alright?"

Bonnie nodded. It was an apt nod, quick and embarrassed. I could tell that she didn't want me to acknowledge what had happened.

"You probably shouldn't work today," I said. "Did you need me to take you home?"

"No. I got it."

I thought of the danger of her driving in her condition. What if she were to pass out at the wheel?

"You know, it probably would be safer if..."

Before I could finish my sentence Bonnie quieted me with an assuring wave of her hand. She stood up steadily, proud, unwavering. Her purse was below the desk. Swooping it up she grabbed her keys and walked out the door like it never happened. I watched from the window as she jumped into her car, turned the ignition, and drove off. I went to the Laundry Room in search of Allan.

"Al?"

"Yeah?" His head peeked out from behind a dryer. He was stocking some blankets on the back wall.

"It's your mom, dude. She fell down in the bathroom about twenty minutes ago. I had to help her to her feet."

Concern rose in his voice. His face reappeared from behind the dryer.

"Where is she now?"

"She left. She drove home."

The concern faded and was replaced with annoyance.

"Ugh, I told her not to come into work. That happened to me last week in my house. I walked up the stairs to get something to eat from the kitchen when I found her sprawled out on the floor. I helped her up and she looked confused, like she didn't know where she was. I don't know how long she had been there, but after helping her up she came to and slowly hobbled into her bedroom."

I sadly and quietly soaked this in.

"Joe?"

"Yeah?"

"Do you still smoke?"

I averaged about half a pack a day. I knew that he knew that I still smoked. I didn't answer back.

"Do you see what's happening to her? If you want to end up like her, keep smoking."

He came off as crude and calloused but I knew that's just how Allan was. He loved his mother. I also knew that deep down though, Al had bitterness towards her. She was a single mother that raised him all of his life, not an easy feat for anyone. I knew he blamed her for those aspects of his life he couldn't control. Most of all, he hated that she had chosen to be a smoker for the last forty years, even though as a child he had pleaded and bargained with her to try to quit, but to no avail.

I turned around and headed out the door to go back to the Office, needing to communicate with Brody on the steps needed to replace Bonnie as the Head Housekeeper for the day. Factoring myself in as a Housekeeper, we had 18 rooms a piece. I was going to try to take on being a Housekeeper and Head Housekeeper so that we could go home at a decent time.

Meth-Arm

"What happened to your arm?" My curiosity got the better of me when I went back to the Office and sat down with Brody in the Break Room after the Bonnie incident to plan the day. Al followed me from the Laundry Room after I filled him in about his mother. He sat in her chair at her desk, eating a cold pork chop.

"I had surgery on it four years ago. I used to be a meth addict for sixteen years and I used needles. My mother introduced me to it."

I stared at his meth-arm.

"Four years ago I had to be rushed to the emergency room because my arm stopped working. My favorite spot of choice was here," as he pointed to the former (and now mostly removed) crook of his left arm. "I injected in the same spot for more than a decade. During this time it got infected, and I didn't know it. After being infected with a staph infection for more than six months, my arm blew out. I had been injecting it the whole time after the original infection happened. When my arm stopped working, it went limp and pain shot up through it from my elbow to my hand. I thought it

was because of a meth overdose; I literally had a needle in me when the pain exploded through my arm."

"Then what happened?" I asked, enthralled.

"Well, I cried out in pain to my friends, who were all wired around me. They were saying stuff like 'don't worry, you probably had an infected needle, it'll go away.' It didn't. A week after my arm stopped working, it turned black. At that point I couldn't ignore the pain anymore, and I had to have one of my friends drop me off at the hospital. He wouldn't stay for fear of being caught with meth on him, or in his system. He merely just drove me there and took off after I walked in through the emergency room doors."

Brody dragged a sheet of paper out in front of him from a stack that he had taken from the Office. It was an audit report. Using his right hand, he started writing on it. As he wrote with his right hand, the fingers on his left hand mimicked and danced exactly in tune with what the fingers on his right hand were doing. His left arm rested on top of the table in clear view. As I stared off into space to process the story Brody had just given me, Al was the first to notice the weird movement on Brody's left arm.

"What's your left arm doing?" There was no respect in Al's voice.

"Oh, that? When they removed the infected part of my arm to save what they could, I was told that several nerves through my upper body would be cross-wired. They not only took 80% of the muscle mass in this area, but they also removed the associated nerve endings with it. My nervous system is still sending the same amount of signals throughout my left arm, but with less nerve endings to give and receive information, it's being 'confused' by the signals also being sent to my right arm."

He turned back to his work. Al left the room and went toward the direction of the Laundry Room. As Brody was busy staring down at his audit work, I caught Al's gaze through the Break Room window before he disappeared out of view. The corners of his mouth were turned upward. I could hear his thoughts. 'Where the fuck do they get these guys?'

I turned to Brody to change the subject from his junkie past to how I was going to approach Bonnie's absence.

"I was thinking of still cleaning the rooms on my chart so that all of us could get out of here at a decent time," I told him. "I'll

still run and check everyone else's rooms. This way we're not stranded here until 8 O' Clock tonight."

"Just don't forget to gather the keys from the vacant rooms at 1pm," he said. "We need to know how many keys are missing, and what locks we have to change." The locks on the doors of the rooms at the Motel Shenanigans, unlike most of the other hotels and motels in the nation, had not yet entered the digital era. The same handles on the doors were the same ones in use since the 1970's. An actual key had to be inserted into the lock to turn it. At 1pm Brody was going to have to spend two hours creating new keys and changing the locks on the doors for those keys that had not been returned. I gathered both my Housekeeping and Head Housekeeping charts and left the Break Room to begin work. It was going to be a long day.

...

When the lunch hour came I was done with roughly seven rooms and had taken two breaks from Housekeeping to run and check how many clean rooms the other Housekeepers had finished. I reported the freshly cleaned rooms into one of the two touch-screen computers in the Office. Fifteen minutes after twelve O'Clock I completed making the bed in 243, finishing my eighth room.

Leaving the room I hovered over my cart in front of the doorway, marking the room as clean on my chart. I heard the jangling of keys to my right. Brody Charmin approached me after ascending the stairwell. A dozen keys procured from vacant rooms dangled from his right, functional hand.

"Because you like cleaning rooms in Housekeeping so much, I'm demoting you. You're no longer the Head Housekeeper of this Motel."

He turned and walked away.

"I told you I was going to get them at 1pm! Everyone has around 18-20 rooms anyway!"

This didn't stop him. He heard me, but he kept his pace, keys jangling.

"WHAT THE FUCK IS WRONG WITH YOU! IF YOU DON'T LIKE IT, YOU CAN CLEAN ROOMS!" I yelled bitterly at him, utterly confused.

My fists were clenched. If he was a graduate of the Motel Shenanigans Managerial University, I was a Rocket Scientist from Vienna. With defiant hatred swimming in my mind, I walked across the top balcony and down the stairwell to the Laundry Room. Allan and Ragnarok were in the Laundry Room listening to Do or Die's "Playa Like Me and You."

"You'll never guess what that junkie son-of-a-bitch just did upstairs," I said to both of them.

Al abruptly laid down the last sheet he was working on. I slammed the door.

"That stupid motherfucker told me because I wasn't gathering keys I'm demoted from Head Housekeeper. We came to an agreement this morning that I'd do both Housekeeping and Head Housekeeping today, because we're understaffed. I told him I'd do it at 1pm!"

"What're you going to do?" Ragnarok asked.

"I don't know."

"You going to quit?" Al questioned.

I was stuck. I wanted my job; sure, it was difficult, but in between working with the remainder of our crew, and going through the crazy adventures, I didn't want to leave. I was beside myself. This kind of treatment I couldn't handle. Besides, I was going to the University of Nebraska – Omaha this upcoming fall, and I needed to save all of the money that I could for school. My parents were broke and couldn't afford shit.

"I…I don't know."

"Don't quit," Al assured me. "You know how he is. You'll be back as a Head Housekeeper in two days, tops."

I reflected on that. "Yeah…you're right."

"Let's go get Hel," he said. "Let's sit down and eat."

All three of us left together to find Hel, the remaining member of our dying quartet of friends employed at the Motel Shenanigans. The seeds of my undying hatred for Brody Charmin, the ex-crystal meth addict, were fully planted on this day.

Hel Leaves

The next day Brody acted like nothing happened. I walked into the Break Room expecting some kind of reprimand or demotion in rank when I saw the already printed Head Housekeepers chart with my name written on the top by Brody's hand. My Head Housekeeper master keys were fixed to the top of the chart.

"What about yesterday?" I said to Brody as he walked into the Break Room.

"What about yesterday?" He asked.

"I thought I was no longer a Head Housekeeper?"

"Well, do what you did yesterday, and it might become permanent."

I had done nothing yesterday. The confusion surrounding the event still imbibed me. I would never trust him again.

"I need you to monitor Hel's rooms carefully. There are reports coming in from new customers that he's not changing their sheets. I've had to issue multiple refunds to different families because they found hair or bodily fluids left behind on his sheets."

Ahhh. Brody needed me to be the point of contact for Hel, to reprimand him, so that Brody could save face. What an asshole. If

Hel would have changed his sheets for all new arrivals (like all employees are supposed to do anyways,) then we wouldn't be having this conversation, and I'd still be a Housekeeper. Brody must have known Hel was my friend. By confronting him about this and forcing him to change, I might be damaging our relationship. Hel didn't take shit from anybody.

Grabbing my chart I left, pissed off. I retreated into 215 (the original hidden caches room,) pulled out the bureau, grabbed a beer, and laid down on the bed. I didn't turn on the TV; I just drank, staring up at the ceiling. What if I just walked out? No, I thought to myself. I had invested the last two and a half years to this place, and didn't have a back-up plan. I needed money for school. My already saved-up funds wouldn't last more than a year. Plus, Allan needed me. I knew he did. He was like a brother. To leave him would be like to leave my family. I couldn't do that. I spent an idyllic twenty minutes downing the warm beer. After it was gone, I grabbed another one. My stomach hurt from the warm beer; my young body hadn't figured out how to process it correctly. I thought I was going to be sick.

Half-way through the second beer I went into the bathroom and poured it out. I barely contained my stomach and fought the urge to profusely vomit. Leaving the room with the empty bottle in my hand, I rounded a corner and threw the bottle into a cylindrical plastic trashcan. I knew what I had to do, heading straight for Hel's rooms. His cart was downstairs by 107. He was outside by the cart, picking up some of the chemical bottles needed to disinfect the room.

"What's up, Joe?"

"Nothin' man. Heads up, Brody knows you're not changing your sheets. He's having me go in after you on every single room to inspect them and make sure they're changed."

The smile left his face. He stood six inches above me, his lip protruding, as the chewing tobacco he had taken that morning clumped underneath his gum line cut into his gums and released nicotine. A small dribble of brown/yellow spit escaped his mouth and dripped halfway down to his chin. He wiped it off with the back of his hand and then spit onto the sidewalk, leaving behind a large black stain. He was as accurate as Josey Wales spitting onto a scorpion from a horse.

"I change my sheets."

I knew that he didn't. In fact, we had discussions weeks before about how funny it was that we didn't. Even I didn't change my sheets sometimes. That occurrence was few and far between, but sometimes compulsively I chose not to. It becomes a problem when you do it with the beds in all of your rooms, as Hel had done.

"I'm just sayin'," I defensively replied.

He didn't say anything else after that. He turned around and went back into 107. Leaving his chart on the cart, I picked it up and checked out what rooms he had already cleaned. 108 and 109 had both been done so far. I went into 108.

The room looked clean. The smell of cigarettes clung to the walls and soured up the air. Without checking the sheets, it looked perfect. I pulled back the comforter and blanket to inspect the sheets.

Son-of-a-Bitch.

They hadn't been changed. One didn't have to be a Head Housekeeper, or housekeeper, to see that. Near the head area, the sheets were stained with what looked to be snot. Yellow trails dotted the linen. I fully pulled back the comforter. Black wisps of human hair covered the entire thing. Even when I made a decision not to change my own sheets, on average I performed this practice once a month, if that. The sheets as well had to look pristine, or close to it. I would never leave sheets like this on the bed for a customer.

Checking the other bed, I found the same thing. Hel had not changed the sheets, although they weren't as bad as the first bed. Still, imprints of a human body could be seen, and even though this bed didn't look as bad as the other bed, it smelled far worse. It reeked of sweat. I tore off the bedding and went back to 107 where Hel was working, knocking on the door. Hel answered.

"Come with me."

Hel followed me quietly but defiantly to 108. Upon seeing the comforter and blanket tossed on the floor, he became enraged.

"What the fuck? I'm not redoing this shit!"

I pointed to the sheets on one bed, and then the other.

"These sheets haven't been changed, dude."

The obvious was glaring out at both of us. The sheets were soiled.

"Listen, motherfucker. I'm not redoing these beds. They were done."

I had to think of some quick action to save my friendship, and my job.

"Listen…I'll remake the beds you've already finished, if the sheets are unchanged. But I'm warning you dude, this isn't me, this is coming from Brody. He said that if he catches you doing this he was going to fire you." (Brody never threatened to fire him, but I hoped this would persuade him.)

Hel stared at me, his lip full of tobacco.

"Alright."

"I'm doing this as your friend, Hel. I want you to keep your job. Be careful and make sure you're cleaning your sheets."

Hel thanked me and left the room. I stood there above his mess, bedding on the floor. It was bullshit I had to clean up after him…but I did like him, after all. During the last senior homecoming dance at Papio, Hel had come over to my house in his blue rusted Ford F-150 and we both took off to the dance, just the two of us, to see what kind of trouble we could cause. We were either thinking of burglarizing or vandalizing other people's cars we didn't like, or trying to pick up some of the chicks coming out of the dance. In the parking lot we didn't get far; Hel made too tight a turn around the corner and jumped a curb, causing his truck bed to sway from side to side. A cop had parked his car by the doors to the cafeteria of the school, and when he saw Hel's erratic behavior he immediately threw his cherries on and drove in for the kill. Hel parked his truck on the side of the curb as the cop navigated and came in behind us. He got out and asked him for his license and registration.

"Do you know why I'm pulling you over?" The cop asked Hel.

"Not exactly, Officer."

"You're driving like your drunk."

"I haven't been drinking, Officer." He was telling the truth.

Hel pulled out his license and the cop took it.

"Registration," the cop demanded.

Hel fumbled around his truck for the registration.

"It's in here somewhere…" he stuttered.

"Maybe it's in here," I said, trying to be helpful. I opened

the glove box and a marijuana pipe (one that I didn't know was in

the vehicle,) glistened in the light of the cop's flashlight.

"It's not in there," Hel said hastily. He slammed the glove

box shut and through his nervous mannerisms, I knew that he knew a

pipe was in there. I had never been in trouble with the law before,

but if the cop searched the vehicle, we could both be ticketed for

possession of paraphernalia.

The cop didn't seem to notice. "I'm going to give you a

warning this time. I can tell you're not drunk. Just get the hell out

of here and don't come back."

The cop left and Hel put it back into drive. "I should have

told you that was in there," he said. We were both counting our

good fortunes to have gotten away.

Hel was slightly a fuck-up, but he was a good friend, and one

you didn't want to lose. I gathered the soiled sheets and carried

them to the Laundry Room, bringing back some fresh sheets so that I

could get to work.

...

A week later Hel quit the Motel. I walked into the Motel Break Room when Brody broke the news.

"I just got a call from Hel. He's not coming in anymore."

Disappointed, I went into the Office and printed off the Housekeeping charts. Our once glorious empire had now been reduced to three employees, which was Allan, Ragnarok, and I. After printing off the charts I laid them out for the Housekeepers and left the Break Room for the Laundry Room. In the Laundry Room I called Hel from the Laundry Room phone.

"Hello?" Hel sounded as if he had just woken up.

"Hel?"

"Yes?"

"Why'd you quit?" I asked.

He paused, but then answered after he figured out who I was.

"Joe?"

"Yeah."

"Because that place fucking sucks, man. I can't do it anymore."

"What about us?"

"What do you mean, 'what about us?'"

"That shit that happened last week. Are we cool?"

Hel answered sincerely. "Oh. We're cool, man. Call me anytime. I got nothing against you at all. Like I said, I fucking hate that place. It steals the soul from you. Joe, you've always been a good friend. I'll talk to you later."

He hung up and I placed the receiver back on the wall. I went back to 215, pulled out a warm beer, and drank by myself.

Bonnie Goes into Hospice Care

"My mom's in Hospice care now, dude."

Allan and I sat at his kitchen table upstairs. We ate some pizza that he had cooked in the microwave.

"What's 'Hospice?'" I asked.

"Basically, it's an organization that helps you die."

"What???"

"Yeah. My mom doesn't have long. She'll be in the hospital for a while, but they're saying what started in her lungs traveled up her spinal cord, and now she has a fist-like tumor in her brain. They've eradicated the tumor in her lungs, thinking that was the only area affected. The tumor in her brain grew unchecked, and now it's too late to operate on it."

"How long does she have?" I asked.

"They don't know. A year at most."

"Goddamnit."

He went back to chewing his pizza slice. I knew Al loved his mother, and that his lack of emotion could be misconstrued as callousness. That's how he was; he wasn't emotional. He was strong.

Later that week I rounded up everyone to go see Bonnie in the hospital. After making several phone calls, I had gotten Turtle, Ken, and Salad to come with me to see her. Turtle pulled up to my house in his Beretta with Salad sitting shotgun and Ken Tarney sitting in the back. I jumped in next to Ken as Turtle offered me a cigarette.

"Thanks," I said to him.

"Just blow the smoke out of the window," Ken annoyingly remarked. He didn't want to smell like us.

We drove out of La Vista and headed towards BM Hospital. Since they had quit the Motel Shenanigans I hadn't seen any of them, and made small talk to pass the time.

"So what's going on with you, Turtle?"

"Me? Nothin'."

"I heard you disappeared for a week strung out on meth," I said.

"Oh, it wasn't a week. It was like four days."

"Turtle, don't take this the wrong way," Ken said, "but when you die, it's just something that I'm going to expect. I'll be sad and all, but I've warned you multiple times that with all of the drugs you take, one day they will kill you."

"Yeah, Yeah," Turtle said passively.

"I know what you're saying," I said to Ken. "I mean, you don't want him to die, but it'll be no surprise when he does, because he's chosen his path."

"Yeah. I don't think I'd cry over it," Ken said bluntly. "We've warned you time and time again, and you still won't change."

"Yeah, I know," Turtle said nonchalantly. He didn't care. He had chosen his lifestyle and was going to die by it.

We rolled into the parking lot. All of us got out and approached the hospital, not knowing what to expect. None of them had seen Bonnie for six months, and I hadn't seen her since she had fallen in the Motel Break Room bathroom. That was around two months ago. I called Allan on my cell.

"We're up here in 316," he said to me on the phone. As stoic as he tried to be in front of me, he always went up to see his mother in his spare time if he didn't have to work.

After getting past the secretary and riding the elevators up to the third floor, there was another secretary we had to pass clearances with. She sat behind thick glass in an office and controlled the button that would open the metal doors that locked down the Hospice section. We were getting ready to enter a death ward. Five excruciating minutes later the doors opened with a large creaking sound. The four of us walked into 316. A nurse tended to Bonnie, gathering up some left over plates of hospital food that had been barely eaten. Al sat in the corner on a chair.

The skeleton that had been Bonnie McCue lay before us. She had shriveled down to about 90 pounds. Her skin that was once taught on her had sagged and gone slack. When we entered in she had been sleeping; Allan sat in his chair, letting her sleep, watching over her. Her eyes slightly opened as she focused on us. They lacked the pride that they contained on the day that she fell and I had helped her up. She recognized us, but fear and weakness were in her eyes now.

"How's it going, Bonnie?" I asked her.

"Good. Tired, mostly. I can't wait until they release me so that I can get back to work."

The others didn't say anything. I think they were too shocked to register that she was going to die.

"Let this teach you all a valuable lesson," Al said aloud, directed at us smokers. Turtle, Ken, and Salad sulked at him in surprise. How could he say something like that in front of his own mother? Only I knew it was a front for his true feelings. If anything I knew Allan was angry that his mother had plenty of chances to avoid reaching this place. It didn't mean that he didn't love her. I went to Bonnie's bedside and sat down on a stool. The other three, Turtle, Ken, and Salad, moved in closer but stayed on their feet.

"So, how're you boys doing these days?" She said. "I haven't seen you guys in a long while."

"We're good Bonnie," different positive affirmations being spoken by the three. She then addressed us individually.

"How're you, Joe? Getting ready for school in the fall?"

"Yeah. I've been accepted into UNO and I'll be getting some grants to do the Writer's Program there."

"You always had a level head on your shoulders," she said. One by one she turned individually to the boys. "What about you, Ken?"

"I'm going to Italy Bonnie. I start Italian language classes at BYU in two months. I'll do that for about three months, before they ship me off to Sardinia."

"Wow. Salad, how about you?"

"I'm working for my dad right now. He's a Union steelworker. I doubt I'll go Union but it's something to do over the summer."

Bonnie's eyes swam in visions, in Life, to the descriptions being told before her. Once upon a time, she had been one of us, all of us, full of hopes, dreams, uncertainty. I imagined her driving around in the back seat of a car with a bunch of other kids, just under 20 years old, passing around a bottle and smoking cigarettes. I thought of the teenage loves she had experienced.

"Turtle?" Her inquiry towards Turtle brought me back to reality.

"Uh, Nothin' much. Just chillin."

Bonnie didn't expect any less. After Turtle's weak answer her eyes changed demeanor and swept over all of us.

"One day...one day you'll all be here...you'll all be here where I'm at today..."

A dead silence filled the room. I broke it without fear, but with factual love.

"You're right. One day, we'll all be where you're at, Bonnie."

Her eyes settled on the ceiling.

"You guys hungry?" I asked all of them. "We should get something to eat. Bonnie, you hungry?"

"Yes! All they give me in here is this horrible hospital food! It tastes like sawdust and oatmeal!"

"I say we go get some chicken. I'll buy you a meal and bring it back for you."

"Promise me you'll be back?"

"Promise."

The five of us including Allan left Bonnie there in her bed.

"I actually have to get going," Al said. "I have to go home and get some homework done."

The four of us went to 114th and Dodge to Carver Market. We ate there. I bought Bonnie a small dark chicken meal to go. It was about an hour later by the time we got back. After the same routine of getting past the secretary checkpoints and through the huge creaking door, Bonnie was half-asleep, and a new tray of grey-green slop was apportioned out to her by her bedside table.

"I thought you guys had forgotten to come back for me," she said.

"I'd never forget about you Bonnie."

I gave the new nurse that was attending to Bonnie's slop the Carver Chicken meal. She set it down and opened it for her, setting it on her chest and giving her a plastic fork. Bonnie's arms shook weakly as she tried to navigate her sweet potatoes and chicken from her plate to her mouth. She took three bites before her head fell back onto her pillow.

"I'm done."

The nurse placed the plastic lid back on the meal.

"Will you save the rest for her?" I said to the nurse. I wanted to make sure Bonnie had all that she could have available to her, in case she was stuck with her bland diet again.

"Of course. I'll put it in the fridge down the hall, with her name on it. There's nothing to worry about."

We said our good-byes to her. Bonnie had already fallen asleep; I'm not sure if she heard us or not by the time we left. We took our cue and went back down the hall and out of the hospital together, towards Turtle's Berretta.

Ragnarok Quits the Motel for Denver

Allan and I sat in the Break Room. I was the Head Housekeeper and arranged multiple charts for the few Housekeepers we did have left (mostly Mexican women, some African immigrants, and of course one for Ragnarok.) The glory days of running the Motel with all of our buddies was over. Every time I came into work now it felt like any humdrum job, full of its own stressors. After going on three years of adventures, the adventures seemed to be waning, and the only thing I looked forward to now was inspecting rooms.

We heard the thumping of a car stereo outside in the parking lot. It was Ragnarok; he had bought a car and a loud stereo system with it. Rag didn't like rap music so when he blasted his music, we could tell the difference. He liked Death Metal; bands such as Cannibal Corpse and all kinds of weird shit, mostly shit without bass, so when it bumped it sounded like guitars and screaming. Sometimes he would drive in blasting hardcore Death Metal with the lead singer screaming, accompanied by a chorus of dwarves chanting in the background along with him.

Ragnarok pulled into a parking stall. He got out and made his way to the Break Room, walking in through the door with his paper sack lunch in his hand. He had a white sheet of paper in the other. After putting his lunch in the refrigerator, Rag turned and gave the white sheet of paper to Brody, who stood in the doorway.

"This is my two week resignation. I'm moving to Denver to go to art school."

Allan and I exchanged glances of disappointment.

"What makes you think you can make it?" Al asked.

"I have to try. Being a designer has always been my dream."

Just like the others Ragnarok was drifting away. It wouldn't be long before I too, or maybe even Allan, would walk away from this place, with the ghosts of our memories stuck in between the walls.

"I'll meet you guys in the Laundry Room," I said. I grabbed my coffee and went out.

In the Laundry Room, I turned on the radio and threw in some Mo' Thugs. I blasted <u>Thug Devotion</u> and sat down in the bin of dirty rags, my thick jeans becoming slightly damp by absorbing the water and chemicals that had stagnated overnight. Sipping the coffee, I tilted my head back and stared at the ceiling. My time at the Motel was coming to an end, and I knew it. Up until now, everyone else quitting was just a mere distracting disturbance. With the exception of Ken Tarney, everyone else had been either a fuck-up or a goofball. Rag, Al, and I were the only real "professional" workers out of our former crew. Losing Rag was a powerful blow that I knew we would never recover from. Besides that, his reasons for leaving were solid; to forward yourself for your own gain, to educate yourself, to experience something outside of what we knew for the last couple of years, surrounded by these cum-stained walls.

The door swung open and both Allan and Ragnarok stepped in.

"Busy at work I see," Al said jokingly.

"You know it," I replied.

Al went to the dirty laundry bin full of sheets and dumped three big armfuls into the washer. He turned it on. Rag got busy gathering towels for his cart.

"Don't worry, Rag. We'll save a job here for you, when you come back."

"Oh, I doubt that," he said matter-of-factly. "My dad is helping me get an apartment out there. This'll be for the long haul. I plan on going out there with him to go apartment hunting next month. Fuck it, it was fun while we were here," Rag finalized.

"And you know," I chimed in, unafraid of change, "we have all been here for what – going on more than three years? How much more time will we spend here, cleaning up after people and listening to people fuck?"

"Yeah, but staying here shows devotion. It shows you have a work ethic." This was Al's argument for staying behind.

"But look at how long we've been here," I counter-argued. "How much more devotion do we have to give?"

Rag grabbed his towels and sheets and headed out for work. Al stood lost in thought and I sat, sipping my coffee and getting my ass wet.

Mailbox Baseball Reunion

"How's the old Motel going?" Turtle asked.

It was shortly after Rag quit. Al, Rag and I sat in the back seat of Turtle's Beretta. Turtle sat up front in the passenger seat, and Pierce Deutsche drove. Turtle was too drunk to drive his own car. Up front, he tightly gripped a baseball bat. He didn't maintain control of it well; it tapped lightly against his window.

"Be careful with that," Pierce said. "You don't want to break your own window, do you?" Pierce Deutsche was an enigma. He had been friends with Turtle since they were kids in elementary school, and had been a stoner and a drunk since early high school. He came from a family of hippie rednecks born out of the heart of La Vista. Pierce had three other brothers, and they were all tough as nails. Nobody fucked with him or his family. As he drove he wasn't wearing a shirt. His unwashed hair billowed out everywhere, and the elastic lining to his underwear peeped out of his jeans, separating itself from the yellow cloth underneath in gaping holes. He was tanned and strong, a product of strength and recklessness.

"Everyone has quit except for me and Al," I told Turtle. "Other than that it's the same old shit. What about yourself?"

"I've been up for a week, same old shit," he said. "Oh wait…THERE'S ONE!"

We were lucky enough to have actually bumped into Turtle and Pierce over at Ragnarok's townhouse previously that night. Al and I had gone over there to drink. While we were walking in we saw Turtle and Pierce across the parking lot, smoking cigarettes with some fifteen year-olds. Turtle held a baseball bat, for unexplained reasons. We invited them in to drink with us and Rag; upon the invitation, Turtle threw the bat in the back seat of his car. In Rag's townhouse, Turtle drank too much beer and could barely walk.

Before that, Turtle had been on a week-long meth binge. He was never at home, and often was driving around with Dickens in the Beretta or in Dickens' rusty Thug Van, smoking meth out of light bulbs together. He spent the last week on the road with little to no sleep, in between the Nebraska panhandle or western Iowa. Through slurred speech he explained to us that he and Pierce were getting ready to play Mailbox baseball. He invited us to go with him to play.

Turtle rolled down his window and sloppily readied the bat for a hit. The rules were simple. In a moving car, you had to hit a mailbox with a baseball bat. If it was knocked off, it was a home run. If it dangled, it wasn't a home run. With the bat and half of his arms out the window, Turtle was ready to swing. The moving wind caught the bat and Turtle's hair, blowing both wildly back. The bat bounced off of Turtle's rear window (the only reason why it didn't crack or break was because he was too drunk and uncoordinated to maintain his strength.)

"Watch it!" Pierce shouted at him.

I saw the mailbox Turtle was aiming for. He still had plenty of time to get to it, although he most likely wasn't going to get a home run. Off to the right of the mailbox and up the driveway to the house I saw the garage door was wide open. Light spilled out and twenty people were standing and walking around, drinking beer from a keg placed in the middle. One large gentleman wore a huge ten-gallon cowboy hat, the kind you see in old westerns.

"OH FUCK!" I screamed. "TURTLE, GET YOUR ASS BACK IN HERE!!!!!!!! THERE'S A FUCKLOAD OF PEOPLE THAT ARE GOING TO SEE YOU DUDE!"

At the mere direction of my voice he collapsed back down onto his seat, almost losing the bat in the process. It swung down and bounced off of his car door, dinging the side.

"WATCH IT!" Pierce angrily repeated.

Turtle brought the bat back into the car and placed it on his lap. I looked behind us at the house full of people and some of them stood now at the edge of the driveway, staring back after us. I wanted to get out of the vehicle immediately. I knew this meant trouble.

Allan must have sensed my thoughts and spoke them aloud.

"You mind if you drop me off? I need to get going," he said.

"Me too," Ragnarok said. "I need to get more drunk."

Pierce drove the Beretta back to Rag's place. On the weekends, Rag's mother and his sister went to his mom's boyfriend's house, giving Rag and his little brother free reign on the townhouse. Almost every weekend involved alcohol. Once we were there, we all got out. Turtle walked around and got into the driver's seat of his car.

"Can you drive, Turtle?" I asked him.

"Yeah."

Rag said his farewell greetings and went into his house. Al walked off towards his white hatchback as I walked back to my mother's rusted-out shitty brown Omni which I had driven over there.

"You mind if I get a ride back home with you?" Pierce asked of me.

"No problem dude."

We got in and I turned the ignition. My mother's car had a rusted out muffler and catalytic converter, so when it drove it sputtered out noxious gases and sounded like shit. As I reversed out, Turtle also reversed. He threw himself into Drive and swerved forward, almost hitting a curb. He steadied himself and lurched out of the parking lot.

"You better follow him," Pierce said. "Just to make sure he gets home."

I drove slowly behind Turtle, weaving in and out of the backstreets of La Vista. Turtle foolishly chose to take the road home right past the house whose mailbox he had just tried to destroy. This time thankfully, the party was over (or the people had taken it inside.) The garage door was shut and no one was outside. We followed him to the stop sign on the road above his house on the hill. He took a detour down a one-way street, right in front of the elementary school that he and Pierce had attended.

"What's he doing?" I asked.

"Probably just smoking a cigarette before he goes home."

"Oh."

As Turtle pulled right I saw the right side of his face. He puffed on a freshly lit cigarette. I stopped in front of the stop sign.

"Should we follow him, or just go home?" I said.

"He's got it," Pierce said. "Just go home."

As soon as Pierce's words had left his lips I took my foot off of the brake. Before I could apply the gas, a cop car flew down with its cherries rolling from the left, down from the hill leading up to Dickens' house. I stomped on the brake to avoid going through the intersection and getting hit by him. He was going 45 mph; like the eagle snatching up a baby prairie dog, the police car swooped in after Turtle. We watched Turtle pull over in front of the school.

"Oh shit," I said.

"Damn," Pierce said.

"What do you want to do?" I asked Pierce.

"Pull in behind him."

I hesitated. "You sure?"

"Yeah."

I took the Omni to the right and slowed down to a stop behind the cop car. At that moment, a second cop car came down the street and parked behind me. Pierce and I were sandwiched in between two police cars. The cop in the first car got out and opened up Turtle's car door. He barked something to Turtle; Turtle got out as cool as James Dean, smoking his cigarette. He nodded to the Officer in agreement to something that was being said, but out of ear shot.

"We should probably say that we're with him. He shouldn't take it all by himself," Pierce said.

"I don't know about that," I replied.

I knew Turtle would tuck tail and run if he could. If I had more of a hand in the destruction of property previously in the night, I would have felt guilty about just wanting to leave. However, I didn't break anything myself, and had wanted to leave them in the first place to avoid this type of situation. Behind us the second cop got out and approached our vehicle, shining his flashlight towards my window to disorient me. I rolled down my window.

"What are you doing here?" The cop asked.

Pierce was silent.

"Nothing," I said. "Just trying to get down the street, past this guy."

"Are you with him? Do you know him?" The cop asked, referring to Turtle.

Before Pierce could interject I answered. "No. No sir, not at all."

"Go ahead and turn around, and get out of here."

"Are you sure about that, Officer? Isn't this a one-way street?" I said.

"I'll let you do it. Just drive on out of here."

The cop approached his partner and like a pair of jackals they circled Turtle. I flipped a U-Turn and drove off, leaving him there.

"I still say we should have said we were with him," Pierce said as I was half-way to his house.

"Well yeah, but that wouldn't have solved anything. Plus, I'm not fucking up my record or getting into trouble with the law over some dumb shit I didn't want to do in the first place."

"It would have been the honorable thing to do," Pierce said.

"There was nothing honorable about tonight, Pierce," I said back.

We drove on in silence back to Pierce's house. His father's truck, a big orange truck with a Confederate flag sticker on the back window, was parked ominously in the driveway.

"Fuck it," he said as he jumped out.

I drove back to my house, wondering how much shit Turtle was going to get into.

The Removal of the Caches

"He's going to be OK. I guess the only thing they're going to charge him with is misdemeanor property damage."

I sipped a beer in 237 with Allan as we watched TV. The day after the Mailbox Baseball incident, I had called Turtle's house and found out that the cops didn't notice he was drunk, and were only charging him with the four or five destroyed mailboxes lying in shambles throughout Turtle's surrounding neighborhood. Even though they hadn't seen him do it, they had probable cause. As it turned out, the house party with the twenty people and the man with the ten-gallon hat had called the police. Turtle's parents were going to get him out of it and place him back on diversion, based on some so-called mental-disorder Turtle had.

"Damn," Al replied after I had told him everything. "I'm glad we left when we did."

"Yeah, no shit."

We sipped in silence. Al was now the main Laundry man in Ragnarok's stead. I was the Head Housekeeper, although now I was in charge of a random group of strangers, mostly Mexican women. Some of my housekeepers were men and women older than me. I had no connection with them; I couldn't just run and grab one of

them the same way I could have grabbed Rag, Turtle, or Hel to run

into a Connecting Room and listen to people fuck. The joy was

squeezed out of my job.

"I have to bring something up to you," Al said.

"Shoot," I replied.

"I need your help in getting rid of most, if not all, of the

Hidden Cache rooms. I want to smuggle everything back to my

house."

"Why now?" I asked him.

"Just because," he said. "Just because."

I could sense the small defeat in his voice. This job wouldn't

last forever. There was no guarantee that I myself would also be

sticking around for too much longer, either. Brody Charmin's mood

swings were too much to bear.

"Of course," I said. "When?"

"Today."

"Sure," I said.

After finishing our beers, we went down to the Laundry

Room together in preparation. Al filled a laundry cart up with

soiled, dirty sheets, and proceeded towards the door. I followed.
We went together first to all of the rooms on the lower level, to all of
our Hidden Cache rooms whose locations we had rehearsed by
memory. Ten or so rooms, filled with hidden cigarettes, beer, or
porn. We entered, deftly swiping our goods and contraband, and
burying it all underneath the sheets in the cart. (In some rooms we
had smaller Hidden Caches of used sex toys like dildos and anal
beads hidden underneath furniture, but we decided to leave it
because of hygienic purposes. Besides, we would never use these
things anyways.) After the first floor was done, we pushed the cart
into the Laundry Room near the back.

"Stay here with it and make sure nobody fucks with it," he
said. "I'm going to bring my car around."

He left me there, hovering over the cart. Within five minutes
the door reopened; he had returned.

"Bring the cart."

I pushed it out of the room after him. His white shitty
hatchback was parked in front of the Motel's electric generator. He
opened the long, curved back door and quickly unearthed our goods,
throwing them into the back. When all of the booze, porn, and

smokes were unloaded, he threw a blanket over the top, and closed the back of the hatchback.

"Take a cart and work on the upstairs rooms. I'm going to swing my car around the back of the Motel by the stairwell in the corner," he instructed me.

"Got it," I said.

I turned around to reach the nearest stairs.

"Oh, and hey," Al continued, "leave 215 alone."

I looked into his eyes and nodded. 215; the original Hidden Caches room. We still had a six pack of beer bottles and four porno mags hidden under the furniture. Obeying his instructions I grabbed a cart from the upstairs Cart Room and wheeled it around to 204. We didn't have as many rooms upstairs that served our purposes as we did downstairs.

I went into 204 and pulled back the bureau. Two beers and a pack of smokes were under it. I picked them up and tossed them into the cart, cleansing the Motel of our perverted ghosts. With each day that lingered our imprint was leaving the walls of this establishment, the memories of our friends sure to fade, and the evidence of our adventures disappearing or being smuggled out in the back of a car that was twenty years older than us.

My Departure

It was midnight and I stood on a lawn with John Mills in the Millard subdivision, in front of a girl's house that John liked. John and I had gone to junior high school together. We hadn't gotten along at first but because of English classes we had together, we developed a close friendship. John was tall and had a piercing in his left ear. His hair was black and combed neatly; we also did theatre together at Papio, working on sets for shows. His father ran Carver's Market across town on Dodge street. We stood in the darkness and I regaled John with former tales of the Motel Shenanigans and how I started to despise the monotony and boredom of my job.

"You should get a job with me," he said. "I can get you one. Hell, my father runs it."

"What would I have to do?"

"It's an entry level position. You'd be scooping food from a buffet onto a plate and handing it out to people. You'd also have to run the cash register. We have separate jobs for cutting the meat for the main entrees and actually making the food. You'd start on the bottom and work your way up."

I knew this was my best way out of the Motel Shenanigans. After three long years, the adventures had stopped, and my love for the place had dried up. Allan was going to hate my decision, I knew he would; but I couldn't do it anymore.

"Yeah. I'll take it."

"Good. I'll talk to my father about it. I actually think we can get you started next week."

The lukewarm wind blew past the treetops and swayed the trees of the suburbs as a group of girls made their way down to us from the house. The most difficult part about leaving the Motel would be leaving Al.

The Announcement

"I'm putting in my two weeks."

Only Brody and I were in the Break Room; Al was in the
Laundry. I unceremoniously handed over my short letter of
resignation, no more than a paragraph long, across the table and over
to Brody.

He didn't register any emotions upon receiving it. Like a
robot he gazed over the letter and then turned around without saying
a word, back into the Office. Whatever Brody thought about me
leaving, I didn't really care. He was also one of the main reasons
why I was leaving; I couldn't stand his asshole nature anymore. My
mind was focused on the hardest part that was yet to come; breaking
the news to Al.

I grabbed my chart and keys and headed for the Laundry
Room. Inside, Al was folding towels and listening to the CD player.
I walked in and sat in the bin with the dirty rags.

"I'm quitting in two weeks," I told him.

He paused only briefly to register this, but then resumed
folding towels. He kept the surprise out of his voice as much as he
could.

"Oh hell, you're saying that now," he said, "but after you leave you'll be back. I'll give you a month before you cave in and try to get your job back."

He was slightly indignant; I sensed it in his voice. I was really the last link that he had to this place. At this point he opened up and spewed forth a barrage of weak scenarios to try to keep me here.

"What are you going to do?" he asked me. "You might as well start applying to all of the fast food jobs that you can. It might take you up to a couple of months to be fully hired on and find one."

"Actually I've already found a job. I'm starting at Carver's Market next week. John Mills got it for me."

He stopped folding and dropped the towel he was holding. My threat had suddenly turned very real.

"What? How?"

"I talked to John a couple of days ago. He got me the job. His dad runs the place."

"Damn it," Al said curtly. "Come with me to strip some sheets from the rooms."

He grabbed the laundry cart and I followed him around the first floor. Like usual, we worked together to check the vacant rooms from the morning's previous vacating customers, looking for booze or anything else forgotten and left over. It must have been an uneventful night; the only things we found were dirty sheets. People actually use Motel bedrooms for sleeping, if not partying. We entered the last vacant room on the first floor when we were almost done. Al drew the blinds and locked the door. I laid down on one bed, he on another. We idly watched TV for a while to pass the time. With some sadness I realized this would be one of the last times I would be paid to just watch TV, hidden away from the eyes of management. Hell, WE were management. Sure, Brody filed the paperwork and made the trips to the bank, but it was US, and all of US before everyone decided to quit, that had ran this place. We had owned it. I had cleaned every single room in the entire Motel more than once. Hell, on days where we had had a moderately sized staff, Al and I had teamed up to paint all of the rooms in the Motel as well. But the saddest thing of all was that I knew I was leaving a chapter in my life I would never be able to walk back into.

"I wonder what this summer is going to be like," he said. "I wonder if we're going to have another prostitution ring come through. Or, how many girls are going to be at the pool."

"You're going to have to tell me about it. I won't be here."

"Yeah, right."

It was then that even though I knew I had told him I was going to quit, he hadn't fully grasped and understood that I was indeed leaving.

"I handed in a resignation letter into Brody this morning, dude. I'm done."

He blinked and stared straight at me.

"No shit?"

"No shit," I replied.

We both went back to watching TV.

Bonnie Passes

My freshman year of college was underway. The last two weeks of my employment at the Motel Shenanigans were more or less uneventful. Nothing too exciting can be said about it. After my last day at the Motel I had begun work at Carver's Market, and in between school during the day and work at night, I was perpetually busy. I saw everyone from the glory days of the Motel less and less.

Months after I had quit the Motel I received a call from Allan. I still lived at my parent's house, and my mom called my name after she answered the phone.

"Joe? Al's on the phone."

I walked into my kitchen and answered it.

"Hey man? How's it going?"

"My mom passed away today, Joe."

I gasped. My hand went to my mouth. Previously Allan kept me informed about Bonnie's general health and I knew it had been worsening. Still, this woman that I had loved, and who had been a second mother to me, was now dead.

When Al said it he wasn't crying, weeping, or even choked up. The only thing that registered was resignation in his voice. I knew that I wouldn't be able to get any other emotions out of him. His mother's illness had matured him already into a young man, and I knew this was the best way he was going to face it. It wouldn't be with tears. Tears wouldn't bring her back.

"Al, you've always been a brother to me. Even though she's gone, you'll always have a family over here. All of us, my parents, my brothers and sisters; we all love you."

I repeated myself twice after I had said it to make sure he understood. Each time I said it, it gained power.

"Thanks, Joe." His reply was sincere. He wasn't going to blubber. I stopped repeating myself when he thanked me, and that's all that I needed.

"Joe, what are you doing tonight?" He asked me. Coincidentally I had the day off from Carver's Market.

"Nothin."

"Come over later. I got to talk to you."

He hung up the phone, leaving me in perfect confusion. What wasn't important enough to talk about on the phone?

My mom walked into the room. I addressed her first.

"Bonnie passed away today."

She groaned.

"Are you OK?" She asked me.

"Yeah…it was coming. Still…ah, forget it." There wasn't really much more I could say.

"If you ever need someone to talk to…" My mother started.

"Oh yeah. I know. Hey…Al wanted me to go over to his house to talk to him about something. I'm going to head over there to see what he wants."

"Go ahead and do that. Right now he needs you more than anything."

I grabbed the keys to my mother's shitty car and drove to the Millard area, to the last house that Bonnie had lived in as a human being before she spent the last year of her life in Hospice care. I drove through the Millard subdivision and parked in front of the school that is across the street from her house; quickly I walked up to their door and knocked on it. Before Bonnie got really sick, they had moved out here; this was around a year and a half ago. She only stayed in the house for about eight months before she had to be committed to the hospital. Al opened the door and let me in.

Following him upstairs, I saw sealed boxes everywhere around the house; he was moving.

"What's going on?" I asked.

"I haven't paid rent for the last two months. I need to get the hell out of here; the landlord keeps calling asking for my mom, asking where his rent money is."

"Holy shit. Doesn't he know that she's been in the hospital for the last year?"

"No. The lease is in her name, and up until two months ago, I was the one making the payments. I figured that if I stopped paying rent for the last couple of months, I could save some serious money. If anyone is going to get dinged for it, I figured it would be my mom, since it's all in her name."

"Damn, isn't that a little harsh?"

I looked into his eyes. They were tearing up. I wished I could have taken my last statement back.

"I don't think my mom cares about her credit score any more, Joe. I'm not too worried about it."

I could see the genuine love in his eyes for Bonnie. There was no denying that. He led me through the house; every room was in a different state of disarray with at least half of the room's contents spilled out either on the ground, or in boxes.

"Where are you moving to?" I asked him.

"I've had my eye on a house at 51st and Q," he said. "It's an older, bigger house. I've already been approved by the landlord there, and plan to move out there next week."

He always had a contingency.

"Hey…why did you call me over here? Did you need help moving to your new house? You know you could have told me that on the phone."

"No. Actually, I need to sit you down for this."

He led me to the kitchen. I sat down at the table and waited patiently for him; he left the room and came back with a pipe and a small bag of weed. He loaded it and we both smoked it together. After getting fairly stoned, he took out his own set of keys on a cheap key-ring. Taking extra care to pull out one key by itself and separate it from the others, he laid it down on the table. The one key of interest that he had pulled apart from the rest pointed accusingly at me like a metal finger from a severed robot.

"What are these?" I asked him.

"These are my keys, Joe. These are the keys to my house, to my car, and this key here," he said as he tapped it with the pipe, "this key is a copy of the Master key of the whole Motel Shenanigans."

I remembered the copy that he had made.

"The Motel has replaced almost every TV in the Motel with brand new working models. The old TVs work fine, but the Motel is piling them up into the Boiler Room by the pool. Brody told me that they're planning on selling them to another motel franchise for a cheap price in the area."

I already knew what he was about to say. And I knew that he knew that my answer was going to be yes.

"Today is a Wednesday, and the usual night watchman at the Motel is only there on Fridays and Saturdays. It's also somewhat slow; not a lot of customers are staying there. Brody is working the desk; he pissed off the last desk clerk and the last clerk walked off. I need your help, Joe. I want to go there, drive in by the pool, pull around to the Horseshoe, and park in front of the Boiler Room. Then, I want to take as many TVs as I can."

"Yes. When?"

"Now."

"Let's do it," I said.

We sat there for no more than five minutes before we stood up and got into Al's white hatchback. His was more elongated than my mother's was; her hatchback was brown and small. Stacked correctly after we lowered his back seat, we could fit about a dozen TVs into the back.

Al pulled away from his house and drove down the street. The car rumbled beneath us loudly. We had been driving down 84th street in this same car a year ago when the whole muffler system fell off the bottom; we played a great risk by bringing the hatchback. The noise itself could be heard for miles. It was only by luck that he hadn't yet been ticketed. Omaha cops were dicks like that.

"What are you going to do at work tomorrow?" I said.

"Actually, I don't have work for the next two days because of mom's passing," he said. "When I go back on the weekend I'm still in Laundry. They got some other lady to be the Head Housekeeper."

We turned right before L Street into the narrow drive that led to the cluster of hotels and motels hidden in the corner of M Street.

We were here. The Motel cringed before us; it did not loom, it did not threaten, it cringed. We used it for so long that we were used to using it. The fucked up dirty rotten rusty stairs, the cheap blue and red paint job on the front. We were not afraid of it. Never were.

"I'm going to drive around the back just to check if the night guard is here today," Al wisely cautioned. "You never know, but it doesn't hurt to check and see, right?"

"Good call," I said.

We drove around the pool to the back, away from the front of the Office.

"What about Brody?" I asked him. It dawned on me that the Boiler Room was right by the front door to the Manager's Apartment; if Brody felt like stepping outside for a smoke, we'd be caught.

"What about him? He's working the desk. He's not going to come out here for anything. If he needs to smoke he'll stick inside the Break Room for that."

"Oh. Got it."

"It still makes me uncomfortable though, to be doing this pretty much on his front doorstep. When we pull up and park, we have to hurry and get this done," he added.

Instead of pulling into the Horseshoe in front of the Manager's Apartment, we pulled around to east side of the Motel and circled around. He parked in front of 104, just out of eyeshot from the Break Room window, reversed, and doubled back. I understood what he was doing.

"Don't want to drive in front of the Office or the Break Room, do you?" I asked him.

"Hell no. Don't want to be seen."

"You know, that's some intelligent thinking right there. How come you almost didn't graduate high school?"

"Shut up, motherfucker," he said back to me.

We pulled back around to the Horseshoe and drove right up front to the Manager's Apartment. My heart raced; his muffler was gone and I was sure Brody heard the engine from outside, even when we entered the parking lot. Al cut the engine; the whirring of his car slowed down and clapped to a stop, like a lawnmower whose safety bar is let go.

"Now," he said. Like Braves stealing horses we leapt from the car. I followed Al to the Boiler Room. He took out the copy of the Master Key, opened it, and before us was a room packed from floor to ceiling with TVs, packed much the way that 119 was stuffed full of pillows. Al picked up the first TV he could find and walked it over to his car. He made it look so easy; his muscles didn't even contract as he lifted. I grabbed one and although it took me a little more effort than what Al had shown, I also gracefully made it to the back of the Hatchback in less than a minute. Within a minute two TVs were already loaded.

We worked methodically. We didn't joke, we didn't speak. After the first two were loaded, we went back for another TV. I recognized the TV that I had grabbed by the cigarette burns on the side of it. It used to belong to a room upstairs above us. A hollow crater marked a burn where the lit end of someone's cigarette had burned its way down to the filter. How it got onto the side of the TV, instead of the top, I'll never know.

Within that second minute we had loaded another two TVs into the back. Al pounced into the back of the Hatchback, rearranging the TVs for more room. He jumped back out and we both took two more. I could see to the back of the Boiler Room; there must have been more than fifty TVs stretching out to the back of the room, next to the boiler and the pool chemicals. The pool vacuum, a hose wrapped up against the wall, hung on a plastic hook and dripped small droplets of water onto the floor. A puddle was collecting under one of the TVs in the back. We wouldn't be taking that one.

We walked the TVs back to the car. I set mine down, Al shoved them in. Like an infant fitting together a puzzle he squeezed them together neatly side by side to conserve room.

"Almost done," he said. It was the first time either of us had said anything since we had opened the Boiler Room door.

"Let's keep going," I said. I hadn't broken a sweat yet. Mixed with adrenaline and weed in my blood, I was high.

We went back two more times for a TV each. After five trips, two TVs each trip, and less than fifteen minutes later, we had the back of Al's white hatchback crammed full. He quietly shut the back of the hatchback. It sagged and almost touched the ground because of the weight.

"Yeah, I need a new car," he said as he noticed my reaction to the sagging undercarriage. "The shocks on this one have went to shit."

He walked over and shut the Boiler Room door. I got into the car waiting patiently for him. After the final task of shutting the door to the Boiler Room, he briskly walked over, got in, and turned the ignition. The car jumped to life, exploding with vibration and sound. Al took the back way out by the pool, going 25 mph, with the back of his car kissing the street.

"Fuck, can't we go any faster than this?" I said worriedly.

"This is the vehicle's top speed," he said, mimicking Arnold Schwarzenegger in Terminator 2. We laughed together, victors of our spoils. In paranoia I looked around us into the different lanes of traffic looking for cops, but there wasn't any.

After our retreat through Millard, we pulled up into Al's driveway.

"You want some of these?" he asked me, beckoning and nodding with his head towards the back seat.

"I'll make some calls to see if anyone else wants one," thinking of a half-dozen friends that might want a cheap TV.

"Don't want one for yourself?"

"Nah. I have a nice one in my room already. And I didn't roll around with you because I wanted a TV. I did it just to do it."

With that we got out of the car. He opened up his garage and I helped him unload the TVs inside and against the wall.

"What are you going to do about these when you have to move?" I asked.

"I'll just drive them to my new house. I still plan on selling a good share of them. I'll give you half, since you earned that much."

"I'll keep that in mind."

I left him in his garage that night. As I got into my mother's brown small hatchback I looked through the closing garage door to see Allan's image fleeting through the door leading into his basement.

All's Well That Ends Well

I awoke with a start. It was a sunny day and I was sleeping in my car in the driver's seat. I was extremely hung-over from the night before, and decked out from head to toe in my Carver's Market regalia. I wore the Carver's Market hat and the blue cotton shirt, but the identifying feature was the gravy and cheese smeared apron that I hadn't bothered to take off. My black khakis were also smeared with food stuffs and chicken grease; my brown work boots were cracked and discolored from being saturated in water and grease constantly. Puddles of water on the floor by the dishwashing sink had contributed to their demise.

I had gotten only four hours of sleep. My stomach churned with sickness from too much Vodka. On this day I had a split shift at the Market, one in the morning, and one in the afternoon. After waking up on my friend Dr. Frank's floor, I had dressed and, reeking of booze, made it on time miraculously to my morning shift. I thought I was going to vomit on people when they were in line for their food. When the morning shift ended, I was too tired to drive home. I passed out behind my wheel in my own car in the parking lot, setting the alarm on my cheap cell phone to wake me up. And here I was now, waking up in the heat of my own car. My window was down and a cool breeze wafted in. I stared through the windshield at the bars and pubs across the street. John Mills' father was inside of the Market, prepping for the dinner hour.

Things were very different now. There were no more shenanigans, at least, none on the same scale as the Motel Shenanigans. My job here consisted of scooping food onto plastic plates. As I stared out of my window at the blue sky I thought of all the adventures that the Motel had offered me over the last three years.

Everyone else had also gotten on with their lives. Ken Tarney was already a year into his missionary work in Sicily. I wrote him often. I had gotten his little brother Lyle a job at the Carver's Market with me. While I wrote to Ken less and less, I became stronger friends with Lyle.

Troy Salad entered the navy. His need to leave Omaha grew in his bones and not even a year after I had left the Motel Shenanigans he was living on an aircraft carrier in the Indian Ocean.

Ragnarok dropped out of the art school that he had attended for a year. I wrote to Rag on a regular basis. In one of his letters he explained to me that they tried to make him draw naked models that they brought into the room; he said he couldn't do it. He wanted to draw only what he was good at, which was monsters, fanciful creatures, and cartoon women with oversized tits getting fucked by six feet cocks. In Omaha, he had a stack of drawings that he had water-colored showing women getting their heads hacked off with axes by demons with huge cocks, while the cocks were still fucking them. Rag worked at a convenience store as a cashier. He got caught pocketing money from the drawer and had to spend three days in jail. After repeatedly watching a drunk Mexican masturbate in front of him in his cell, he was released and got a job as a jizz mop janitor at a porno store. He was now on probation in Colorado and couldn't leave the state until next year.

Hel Samwig joined the army and was proudly serving his country in Iraq. I never heard from him again.

Dickens still lived at home in his parents' house in La Vista. He got a job at a bank as a teller. The only drug he touches now is weed. He's got two kids. I see him about once every six months.

Mac Whiane, who worked at the Motel for only a week, now lives in Florida. He and his wife have a daughter and they both work at a consignment warehouse, filling orders over the phone for plumbing companies.

The only thing keeping Turtle alive is his parents. The meth rock he found in that Motel on that fateful day has ensnared him ever since. No one else wants anything to do with him. He moved in with Allan for a short while but Al kicked him out for stealing weed from him. Turtle spends his weeks high on meth, traveling Omaha and the greater Midwestern area, always in search of more meth or scrap metal to take to the scrap yards. When he hasn't slept in a week and needs a place to crash, he'll drive back home to his parents and they'll take him in. He'll go through what he calls a "meth coma," being dead asleep for up to 48 hours, before waking up, raiding the fridge, and leaving again. His Beretta broke down so his parents bought him a huge nice green truck. Just like the Beretta the truck is now mangled, the insides choked with trash, clothes, and cigarette butts. The metal frame of the truck has seen countless accidents, both with cars and interstate medians as he side-swipes them when he falls asleep at the wheel. He and the truck are still alive, floating down one of the many highways that you may be driving down.

Allan got a job at a construction company, and now is working towards a Journeyman Electrical Apprenticeship. He ended up dating and being engaged to my own sister, who is a tattoo artist. I still love him. He'll never stop being my brother.

I opened the door to my car. My stomach felt better, as my system had repaired most of the damage from the alcohol. I walked into Carver's Market, washed my hands thoroughly, and got ready for the dinner rush.

- March 2023

Joseph William Simmons was born in Omaha in 1981. He graduated from the University of Nebraska – Lincoln in 2004 with a Bachelors in Film Studies with minors in Asian Studies, Japanese, and theatre. In 2006 he received a teaching job overseas and moved to Shinkamigoto, Japan. He lived there for 3 years, learning the Japanese language while traveling Asia and Australia. In 2009 he returned to the States and became employed at a money processing job for 3 and a half years. One day after going to work at this desk and cubicle job, he looked out the window, reflected on his future, got up, and walked out. After this he never returned to the lifestyle of corporate America.

In 2013 he graduated from the University of Nebraska's graduate college with a Masters in Creative Writing with an emphasis in Literary Non-fiction. Needing work to pay off his ridiculous, over-inflated, and life destroying student loans, he turned to industrial carpentry. After working for five years as a commercial carpenter, Joseph moved to Wyoming and tried his luck as a roughneck on an oil rig; after nearly being decapitated on the oil rig floor, Joseph moved back to Omaha and has since worked for the Electrical Union.

In his spare time he produces and acts in independent films, most of them made in the Omaha and Council Bluffs area. Once in a while his name will be attached to film projects on the west coast and overseas in the United Kingdom after paying meager amounts to fund microbudget horror and comedy films.

Made in the USA
Monee, IL
04 September 2023

42122752R00164